GET A GRIP ON YOUR EMOTIONAL INTELLIGENCE

ENHANCE RELATIONSHIPS AND ACHIEVE SELF-MASTERY

KENNY LEE

© **Copyright 2024 - All rights reserved.**

The content contained within this book may not be reproduced, duplicated, or transmitted without direct written permission from the author or the publisher.

Under no circumstances will any blame or legal responsibility be held against the publisher or author for any damages, reparation, or monetary loss due to the information contained within this book, either directly or indirectly.

Legal Notice:

This book is copyright protected and is only for personal use. You cannot amend, distribute, sell, use, quote, or paraphrase any part or the content within this book without the consent of the author or publisher.

Disclaimer Notice:

Please note that the information in this document is for educational and entertainment purposes only. All efforts have been made to present accurate, up-to-date, reliable, and complete information. No warranties of any kind are declared or implied. Readers acknowledge that the author is not engaged in the rendering of legal, financial, medical, or professional advice. The content in this book has been derived from various sources. Please consult a licensed professional before attempting any techniques outlined in this book.

By reading this document, the reader agrees that under no circumstances is the author responsible for any direct or indirect losses incurred as a result of the use of the information contained within this document, including, but not limited to, errors, omissions, or inaccuracies.

CONTENTS

Foreword	7
Introduction	9
1. UNRAVELING EMOTIONAL INTELLIGENCE	13
Emotional Intelligence Constructed	14
Origins of Emotional Intelligence	15
The 4 Pillars of Emotional Intelligence	22
Emotional Intelligence and Your Success	26
Chapter Recap	29
Action Items	29
Get-A-Grip Emotional Intelligence Assessment ©	31
2. SELF-AWARENESS – YOUR JOURNEY TO SELF-DISCOVERY	33
Introspection and Self-Reflection	34
Recognizing Emotions	44
Emotional Awareness Tools	49
Chapter Recap	51
Action Items	51
Tools for Further Assessment	53
3. SELF-MANAGEMENT: EMOTIONAL REGULATION AND CONTROL	55
The Science of Self-Management	57
Mastering Self-Management and Emotional Regulation	64
Developing Emotional Resilience	71
Chapter Recap	74
Action Items	75
4. SOCIAL AWARENESS: EMPATHY, COMPASSION, AND UNDERSTANDING OTHERS	81
The Essence of Empathy	82
Exercise Your Empathy	86
Compassion in Action	91

Chapter Recap	92
Action Items	93

5. RELATIONSHIP MANAGEMENT: MASTERING AND APPLYING SOCIAL SKILLS

	95
The Art of Communication	97
Effective Communication	98
Nonverbal Communication	103
Conflict Resolution	107
Chapter Recap	109
Action Items	109

6. MOTIVATION AND EMOTIONAL INTELLIGENCE

	113
The Drive Within	114
Intrinsic vs. Extrinsic Motivation	115
Cultivating Self-Motivation	117
Setting and Achieving Goals	119
Chapter Recap	122
Action Items	123

7. LEADERSHIP AND EMOTIONAL INTELLIGENCE

	127
Emotional Intelligence in Leadership	128
Leadership Styles and EI	129
Building Effective Teams	132
Leading with Empathy	134
Chapter Recap	138
Action Items	138

8. EMOTIONAL INTELLIGENCE AND LIFELONG LEARNING

	141
The Learning Mindset	142
The Growth Mindset	143
Learning From Experience	147
Continuous Improvement	148
Chapter Recap	152
Action Items	152

9. EMOTIONAL INTELLIGENCE AND MENTAL HEALTH

	155
Emotional Well-Being	156
Emotional Intelligence and Mental Health	157
Managing Stress and Anxiety	160

Chapter Recap	162
Action Items	162
10. EMOTIONAL INTELLIGENCE AND TRANSFORMATION	165
Transforming Life and Leadership	166
Self-Mastery and Emotional Intelligence	168
Achieving Balance and Harmony	170
Chapter Recap	171
Action Items	171
Conclusion	173
Appendix 1 – Get-A-Grip Emotional Intelligence Assessment ©	179
Appendix 2 – Management of Anxiety, Anger, Sadness, and Depression	191
References	201

FOREWORD

The concepts in this book about Emotional Intelligence, EI, have been integral to my journey through life. I know from my 25 years in the military and my experience as a life coach, registered nurse, and caregiver that your EI puts you in the driver's seat of your life's direction, both as it has come naturally to you and through what you have learned over your lifetime. The 4 Pillars of EI are the foundation of your self-mastery and relationships with those around you.

If you like this book and learn from its values, please leave a review on Amazon, Audible, or wherever you may have obtained this copy. I humbly appreciate it, and so will the readers who choose to follow you.

Just click on the link below or scan the QR code here:

[https://www.amazon.com/review/review-your-purchases/?asin=B0CZ7V6QCD]

As a BONUS... Additional exercises along with news and updates to help you Get A Grip On Your Emotional Intelligence are available to you FREE.

Just send me an email at: KennyLeeBooks@gmail.com

Use the subject line: "Get A Grip EI Stuff" and I will send you a bonus set of exercises along with updates for your Emotional Intelligence journey into your future.

Look deep inside. I thank you. And you will soon thank yourself.

Your Life. Your Health. Your Journey... Take Action!

~ Kenny Lee

INTRODUCTION

Have you ever wondered why some people have more control over their lives than others? How they deal with stressful situations effectively and keep a check on their emotions? How they always seem to say or do the right thing to help others when a crisis hits?

Emotional intelligence (EI) is the ability to identify, understand, and regulate one's emotions and empathize with others. A high emotional quotient (EQ), on which EI is based, contributes to stronger, healthier personal and professional relationships. People with high EI not only manage to navigate through life more easily but are also more successful.

Studies show that 82% of global companies now use EI tests to hire for executive positions. Additionally, 72% of these companies test middle management applicants for EI, while 59% test EI when hiring for entry-level positions. Without developed EI, your chances of gaining your desired job or position could be considerably reduced (Castillo, 2023).

Emotional intelligence improves your understanding, awareness, and ability to deal with situations regardless of their challenges. EI helps you work with people cohesively, reduces stress and conflict, and improves overall life quality for you and those around you.

Emily's story is a case in point. She dreaded the thought of getting on an airplane. Whenever she needed to fly somewhere, the days leading up to the travel were scattered and stressful, and she was on edge both at work and at home with her family. Her work suffered; she always had an excuse not to go on business trips. Her family couldn't plan vacations that involved air travel.

Emily isn't the only one with this fear. It is common even for frequent flyers to have jittery nerves before a flight due to combinations of stress and anxiety, irritability, and unrealistic fears and assumptions. Often, we don't realize the impact our reactions and feelings have on ourselves and the people around us. Whether it is a fear of flying, a stressor, or a problem in your personal or professional life, getting a grip on your emotional intelligence bolsters your awareness and management through these issues and your relationships as you work through the obstacles in life.

Emily and her husband, John, sought counseling for her fear of flying. John himself had mild anxiety with flying and understood some of what Emily was experiencing. Through work with their therapist, they learned that her situation compounded upon itself, and as travel dates and flights approached, the molehill became a mountain. Small interventions were learned and practiced to alleviate the symptoms she experienced and to prevent escalation.

They planned a vacation getaway to Hawaii. Emily and John used the calming exercises of focused breathing and meditation to relieve stress and anxiety as departure day approached. As they drove to the airport, she verbalized and discussed her current feelings with John and used visualization and positive affirmations to build her confidence. As the seat belts were fastened, Emily repeated a short, positive mantra and used controlled breathing. John held her hand as they taxied for takeoff. Visualization of a smooth flight did not keep her from squeezing John's hand tightly as they rolled on takeoff, but her anxiety was controlled. As the flight climbed away, Emily looked out the window at the receding city, mountains, and blue ocean. Her visualization exercise had come to life. The view, the flight, her inner being had a clarity that she never thought possible while flying.

"It's going to be a great trip," said Emily.

John smiled, squeezed her hand, and agreed.

THE OBJECTIVE OF THE BOOK

This book focuses on helping you understand how to build your 4 Pillars of Emotional Intelligence: Self-awareness, self-management, social awareness, and relationship management. You will identify your strengths, weaknesses, triggers, and motivations, then develop a plan with defined goals so you can work on each of these areas and strengthen your pillars.

Have a dedicated notebook or journal to jot down notes and to put on paper your thoughts, goals, and answers to the Action Items. Track your progress.

The end objective: Get a grip on your emotional intelligence, reinforce your 4 Pillars of EI, enhance your relationships, and achieve self-mastery.

"It is very important to understand that emotional intelligence is not the opposite of intelligence, it is not the triumph of heart over head— it is the unique intersection of both."

DAVID CARUSO

CHAPTER 1
UNRAVELING EMOTIONAL INTELLIGENCE

Let's get into the concept of emotional intelligence, EI, and how it affects our daily lives. Before we begin, let's ponder over a few questions:

- How does the continuous cultivation of your emotional intelligence contribute to your lifelong personal and professional growth, learning, and development?
- How can you practice emotional intelligence to achieve a sense of balance, resilience, and emotional stability in the face of challenges?
- What role does your level of emotional intelligence play in building and maintaining healthy, positive relationships with peers, supervisors, subordinates, friends, and family?

To better understand these questions and help you find the answers, let's first look at the 4 Pillars of EI and how the EI theory evolved and became a mainstream measure of our social and emotional being.

EMOTIONAL INTELLIGENCE CONSTRUCTED

Consider the 4 Pillars of Emotional Intelligence, the construct of your EI:

- We perceive ourselves through self-examination, assessment, evaluation, and reassessment. We gain learning, knowledge, understanding, and wisdom about ourselves to manage our thoughts, desires, motivations, emotions, and actions to gain self-mastery. These **personal competencies** make up the first two pillars of EI:
- **Pillar 1, Self-Awareness** – the understanding and awareness of your own feelings and emotions.
- **Pillar 2. Self-Management** – the capacity to guide, control, and refine our own emotions and behaviors.
- We use our personal competencies to develop our recognition and understanding of the emotions of others and learn to know and feel empathy toward others around us. We show this empathy, express ourselves, and act toward others to build, maintain, and enhance healthy relationships. These **social competencies** make up the second two pillars of EI:
- **Pillar 3, Social Awareness** –the recognition and understanding of emotions in others.
- **Pillar 4, Relationship Management** – the building, development, and nurture of our relationships with others.

	1) Self-Awareness	2) Self-Management
Personal Competencies		
Social Competencies	3) Social Awareness	4) Relationship Management

The 4 Pillars of Emotional Intelligence

The development of these four Pillars is the foundation of your emotional intelligence. EI directly contributes to how you deal with stress, communicate, and understand what others are feeling. High EI enhances problem-solving skills and contributes to building stronger relationships, performing better in your career, and learning to connect with your feelings to transcend your intentions into actions and focus on what's most important.

Next, let's look at the evolution of this model for EI that began a century ago.

ORIGINS OF EMOTIONAL INTELLIGENCE

The origin of EI can be traced back to psychologist Edward Thorndike. He first proposed the concept of social intelligence in 1920, which he defined as "the ability to understand and manage men and women, boys and girls, and to act wisely in human relations" (Kihlstrom & Cantor, 2011).

By the 1930s, psychologists built upon this concept and developed our understanding of social intelligence. P.E. Vernon describes this concept as (*'Social Intelligence' in Research*, n.d.):

... reflected in the general ability to get along with people in general, social technique or ease in society, knowledge of social matters and susceptibility to stimuli from other members of a group, as well as insight into the temporary moods or underlying personality traits of strangers.

The 1940s and 50s saw the rise of humanistic psychology, a time when American psychologist Abraham Maslow began to consider psychological health an important basic need for humanity. Maslow became famous for developing Maslow's Hierarchy of Needs, which begins with physiological needs and transitions to safety, love and belonging, and esteem before the peak of self-actualization (Celestine, 2023).

SELF-ACTUALIZATION
become the most one can be

ESTEEM
respect, self-esteem, status

LOVE AND BELONGING
friendship, intimacy, family

SAFETY NEEDS
personal security, health, employment

PHYSIOLOGICAL NEEDS
air, water, food, shelter,

Maslow's Hierarchy of Needs

In his 1983 book *Frames of Mind*, Harvard professor and psychologist Howard Gardner spells out his theory on there being multiple intelligences. He lists eight different types of intelligence:

1. Spatial: visualizing the 3D world.
2. Naturalist: understanding nature and living things.
3. Musical: discerning sounds, pitch, timbre, tone, and rhythm.
4. Body/Kinesthetic: coordinating mind with body.
5. Linguistic: finding the right words to express oneself.
6. Logical/Mathematical: quantify, hypothesize, and prove things.
7. Intrapersonal: know and understand yourself, your feelings, and what you need.
8. Interpersonal: sensing other's motivations and feelings.

Gardner actively continues his research, suggesting there are other candidates to include in addition to these original eight. Areas considered by Gardner are spiritual, existential, and moral intelligence (Marenus, 2023).

While Gardner promoted his work in the field, Wayne Payne published his doctoral thesis in 1985 at Union Grad School in Ann Arbor, Michigan. Payne introduced the term "Emotional Intelligence" as it "involves relating creatively to fear, pain, and desire." This thesis is the first academic acknowledgment of EI as a stand-alone phenomenon (Payne, 1985).

Also in 1985, the Israeli psychologist Reuven Bar-On proposed for his doctoral thesis a quantitative technique to measure the Emotional Quotient just as one can measure the Intelligence Quotient (IQ). Bar-On addresses emotional intelligence as part of this thesis (Bar-On, 2004).

In 1990, Peter Salovey and John Mayer published their first article on emotional intelligence. This article was published in the journal *Imagination, Cognition, and Personality* and was the turning point for the emergence of the concept of EI (Salovey & Mayer, 1990).

Referencing Salvoy and Mayer's work, Daniel Goleman published a book in 1995 titled *Emotional Intelligence: Why It Can Matter More Than IQ*. This book brought EI to the mainstream, and EI theory and application developed at an exponential rate in different fields, including science, psychology, academia, and business. Goleman continued his research and in 1998 proposed five domains in EI: Self-awareness, self-regulation, motivation, empathy, and social skill. After continued study, Goleman combined motivation and self-regulation and revamped his model in 2002 to the present 4-domain vision of EI. (Goleman, 2023). We address that model here as the 4 Pillars of Emotional Intelligence.

Essentially, your personal competencies are your perceptions of yourself – self-awareness – and your actions related to your self-awareness – self-management. Likewise, your social competencies are your perceptions of others – social awareness – and your actions related to your social awareness – relationship management.

	Your Perceptions	Your Actions
Personal Competencies	**1) Self-Awareness**	**2) Self-Management**
Social Competencies	**3) Social Awareness**	**4) Relationship Management**

The 4 Pillars of Emotional Intelligence

This is the model we will explore to give you the tools to see where you stand and how you can make changes and improvements to get a firm grip on your emotional intelligence. We will look now at how EI and EQ are measured and then expand on the 4 Pillars and why EI is important to you.

Measuring Emotional Intelligence

So how do we measure your emotional intelligence, EI? What is your emotional quotient, EQ?

BarOn Model and EQ-i

In 2004, the BarOn Emotional Quotient-Inventory (BarOn EQ-i) test was born. Based on over 20 years of research by Dr. Bar-On and tested on over 110,000 individuals worldwide, the BarOn EQ-i measures emotional and social intelligence behaviors as reported by those tested. Research based on EQ testing shows that EI is a key factor in determining success in the lives of those individuals.

The EQ-i tests and measures 133 items and yields scores in these areas:

- **Intrapersonal:** Consists of self-actualization, emotional self-awareness, assertiveness, self-regard, and independence.
- **Interpersonal:** Made up of social responsibility, empathy, and interpersonal relationships.
- **Stress management:** Regards impulse control and stress tolerance.
- **Adaptability:** Deals with problem-solving, reality testing, and flexibility.
- **General mood scale:** Measures happiness and optimism.

The BarOn EQ-i received updates in 2011 and is now referred to as the EQ-I 2.0, which serves today as the standard for quantitative measures of social and emotional intelligence.

Mayer and Salovey's Model and EI

Mayer and Salovey's work in the 1990s developed the model of EI which consists of four branches.

- **Branch 1:** Perceiving, recognizing, and understanding emotions in yourself and others.
- **Branch 2:** Using emotions to think clearly and effectively.
- **Branch 3:** Understanding emotions and the ability to analyze trends and understand outcomes.
- **Branch 4:** Managing emotions to be socially aware, know yourself, and achieve specific goals.

In 2004, Mayer and Salovey teamed up with David Caruso to develop the Mayer-Salovey-Caruso Emotional Intelligence Test (MSCEIT). This abilities-based test uses Mayer and Salovey's four-branch model as a measure in 141 questions. Results are broken down into the EI branch components of perceiving, facilitating, understanding, and managing emotions. The MSCEIT uses common scenarios and normative sampling to ensure valid results (*The Mayer-Salovey-Caruso emotional intelligence test*, n.d.).

Testing Variations Today

A number of companies have built their own models for testing EQ/EI. At the foundation of all of these tests are the two testing platforms of the BarOn EQ-i and the MSCEIT.

The EQ-i 2.0 test of today provides clinicians, employers, educators, and researchers with a measurement of emotional intelligence, emotional health, and overall psychosocial wellness. It is used for exploration, evaluation, and treatment. A branch of this test is the EQ 360 test, which assesses EI for leadership.

The MSCEIT for adults has been adapted to test youth in the MSCEIT-YRV version of the test. MHS of Toronto, Ontario (Canada) owns the copyright and is the sole distribution point of the MSCEIT.

An Assessment of Your Emotional Intelligence

Action Item questions at the end of this chapter will give you the flavor of content that defines your EI. You will consider these questions first, then take an assessment to give you a baseline for your Emotional Intelligence.

You will be assessed on your 4 Pillars of Emotional Intelligence, defined below. You can use the results of this test to build and improve your EI for better relationships, both personal and professional, and achieve the level of self-mastery you desire.

How important is EI to you and your life? Let's take a look.

THE 4 PILLARS OF EMOTIONAL INTELLIGENCE

Pillar 1) Self-Awareness

Self-awareness is the conscious knowledge of your own character, feelings, motives, and desires. It is your ability to think about yourself, to reflect on personal thoughts, feelings, and behaviors, and to recognize how you are perceived by others. This metacognitive capacity enables you to examine your own internal states and to make judgments about yourself that are separate from your environment and experiences. For example, through self-awareness, you can identify emotions like happiness or anger within yourself, understand why these emotions have arisen, and anticipate how they might affect your actions.

At a deeper level, self-awareness is not just about recognizing emotions or thoughts but also understanding your own cognitive biases, strengths, and weaknesses. It includes the recognition of your own personality, personal values, and beliefs. With high self-awareness, you can often see how your thoughts and emotions play a role in your behaviors and you are better equipped to handle challenges and build strong relationships. This awareness is a crucial component of your emotional intelligence and is thought to be a cornerstone of mental health and well-being.

Developing your self-awareness is a lifelong process that can be enhanced through practices like mindfulness, reflective journaling, and feedback from others. It is not a static state but a dynamic quality that can improve with intention and practice. As you become more self-aware, you will tend to make more conscious choices that align with your authentic self, which can lead to greater fulfillment and purpose in life. Moreover, self-awareness allows you to adapt more readily to change, be more empathetic to others, and effectively manage your social and personal roles in our complex, diverse societies.

Pillar 2) Self-Management

Self-management is essentially like being the CEO of your own life. It's about taking charge of your actions, emotions, and thoughts in a way that propels you forward. Think of it as having an internal compass that guides you through your daily routine, goals, and challenges. It's about making deliberate choices rather than just reacting to whatever life throws at you. For instance, it's choosing to wake up early for that jog, despite really wanting to hit the snooze button, or managing to keep your cool in a stressful situation at work. It's the art of steering your own ship, keeping yourself on track, and not getting swayed by every passing wave.

This skill encompasses a range of smaller but crucial skills like time management, emotional regulation, and personal productivity. It's about setting up structures and systems that help you stay organized and focused. Imagine it as having an inner planner that helps you break down your big goals into bite-sized, achievable tasks. It also involves being aware of your emotional state and knowing how to handle it. Say you're feeling super annoyed about something; self-management is taking a moment to breathe and think it through instead of immediately reacting and potentially making things worse. It's the ability to self-motivate and keep pushing forward, even when things get tough or boring.

But here's the kicker: self-management isn't about being perfect. It's about being adaptable and resilient. Life is unpredictable – one day, everything's smooth sailing, and the next, you're hit with a curveball. Good self-management means being able to pivot and adjust your plans without losing sight of your overall goals. It's also about being kind to yourself when things don't go as planned, learning from your experiences, and not beating yourself up over mistakes. In essence, self-management is the ongoing process of developing and maintaining a balanced, goal-oriented, and emotionally stable approach to life.

Pillar 3) Social Awareness

Social awareness is understanding and navigating social contexts with sensitivity and empathy. It's about being attuned to the feelings, thoughts, and experiences of others, even when they may not be explicitly expressed. Picture it as having a finely tuned social antenna that picks up the nuances of body language, tone of voice, and even unspoken emotions in a group setting. This understanding extends beyond individual interactions, encompassing broader societal dynamics, cultural norms, and diversity. With high social awareness, you can read a room effortlessly, understanding when to offer a word of encouragement, when to listen, or when to change the subject to ease tensions.

This skill isn't just about being perceptive; it's also deeply linked to empathy. It involves recognizing and respecting the perspectives and feelings of others, even if they differ from your own. For instance, in a conversation, someone with strong social awareness will not only listen to what is being said but also pay attention to what's left unsaid, tuning into hesitations or emotional shifts. They are the ones who can put themselves in someone else's shoes, understand their point of view, and respond with compassion and sensitivity. This empathy extends to a broader understanding of social structures and inequalities, making socially aware individuals more conscientious and considerate in diverse settings.

Moreover, social awareness is integral to effective communication and relationship-building, both in personal and professional realms. It enables you to navigate complex social environments, build strong networks, and develop meaningful relationships. In the workplace, for instance, it translates to better teamwork, conflict resolution, and leadership. It's about making everyone feel valued and understood, creating an inclusive and supportive environment. In essence, social awareness blends observation, empathy, and a keen understanding of social dynamics to foster healthier, more successful interactions and relationships in all areas of life.

Pillar 4) Relationship Management

Relationship management is an essential skill for navigating the complexities of personal and professional interactions effectively and harmoniously. At its core, it's about establishing and maintaining positive connections with others, whether in friendships, family, work, or casual acquaintances. This involves not just initial rapport-building but also the ongoing nurturing of these relationships. You can foster trust and understanding, communicate clearly, and show consistent respect and empathy towards others. You are adept at not just sharing your own thoughts and feelings, but also actively listening and responding to those of others, thereby creating a two-way street of mutual respect and understanding.

In practice, effective relationship management often involves a degree of conflict resolution and negotiation skills. Disagreements and misunderstandings are inevitable in any relationship, but managing these situations with patience, a calm demeanor, and effective communication can prevent them from escalating. It also means being able to give and receive constructive feedback, helping others to grow while also being open to personal growth. It's about finding a balance between asserting your own needs and accommodating those of others, creating a harmonious and supportive dynamic. As you excel in relationship management, you are often seen as reliable, trustworthy, and empathetic – qualities that strengthen any relationship.

Beyond the interpersonal level, relationship management is crucial in professional settings for leadership, team building, and customer relations. As a leader skilled in this area, you will motivate and inspire your teams and foster a positive and productive work environment. You understand the strengths and weaknesses of your team members and can delegate and guide accordingly. In customer-facing roles, relationship management skills enable you to connect with clients, understand their needs, and build loyalty over time. This skill is not just about being friendly or a 'people person'; it's about intentional and consistent efforts to understand, connect with, and positively influence those around you.

EMOTIONAL INTELLIGENCE AND YOUR SUCCESS

Emotional Intelligence is an essential factor in the success of your personal and professional relationships. It also enables you to achieve your goals and become more successful. How you respond to situations in life impacts your relationships with others. You'll interact with diverse groups of people and situations during your journey. Some people will take you by surprise; some situations may shock you. But with well-developed EI you can empathize, relate, and understand those people and situations. Irrespective of what life throws your way, you can be composed and prepared, showing compassion and dealing with the changes.

Being emotionally intelligent helps you reason with your emotions and understand their impact on your relationship with others. Not only will you be able to focus on and motivate yourself to do certain tasks, but you'll also be able to interact with and inspire others around you by creating a happy environment, which leads to success. Here are a few reasons why EI will make you more successful:

Better Understanding

Whether in your personal or professional life, communication is critical. Communicating effectively and providing constructive feedback by motivating people and still showing empathy towards them helps you go on the right path.

Understanding Personal Emotions

It's common for people to have their ups and downs, but being able to understand when someone is having a bad day and help them through it creates a strong bond. This skill, in turn, leads to success in the long run.

Better Efficiency

Empathizing with people helps you understand what they're thinking. It also enables you to explain tasks to them more efficiently, leading to a streamlined workflow.

Impact on Mental Health

Emotionally intelligent people are at a lesser risk of being anxious or depressed. EI has a strong positive impact on these disorders and will allow you to stay in control of your emotions. If you suffer from anxiety, depression, or other mental health issues, EI will help you avoid acute flare-ups and mitigate any chronic conditions you may have.

Correlation With Leadership Skills

An emotionally intelligent person understands how to be an active listener, patient, empathetic, and positive—all desirable skills for leadership roles. Harvard Business School sees EI as "one of the most sought-after interpersonal skills in the workplace," with 71% of employers valuing EI over technical skills (Landry, 2019).

Relevance in Conflict Resolution

Conflicts can create multiple problems in your personal and professional life. Being able to manage conflict efficiently is a sign of a high EI. When you can regulate and control your emotions while recognizing the emotions of others, you will have a basis to work with to resolve conflict. While there is often no way to avoid a confrontation, you can employ your EI to effectively handle the situation without letting it blow out of proportion, and you will be much more likely to reach a resolution that is agreeable to both parties.

Influence on Overall Well-Being

There's no denying that positive well-being and EI have a strong correlation. Your emotional intelligence positively impacts you and the people around you. You will be more aware of the situations in life, you will experience more satisfaction, and you will gain higher self-esteem and self-acceptance. These qualities lower your risk of depression and stress and increase your likelihood of being able to thrive in any situation. You will empathize and connect well with the people around you and build stronger successful relationships.

CHAPTER RECAP

Emotional intelligence might seem like a simple term, but there is a lot involved in assessing your EI and building upon what you already have to achieve success. In this chapter, we defined EI and looked at its origins and evolution. We covered the four Pillars of EI, discussed the ways EI is measured, and discussed the importance of emotional intelligence to your life and its relationship to your success.

We have scratched the surface and given you a basic understanding at this point. The action items below will give you the baseline on your own EI and show you your areas of strength and areas for improvement. The remaining chapters will dive into more details to reinforce and improve your EI so you can achieve success in self-mastery and your relationship with others.

ACTION ITEMS

Now that you've got a basic understanding of what EI is all about, take some time to assess your EI and see where you stand. These Action Items are very important for you to gain a picture of where you are at with your emotional intelligence. Take the time now to go over these before continuing further. It will pay you dividends in the end.

First, making entries in your notebook/journal, please answer the following questions honestly:

- How well do you control your thoughts? Are you able to regain focus when life around you gets a little chaotic? Can you put away negative thoughts, accept them, and move on?
- Do you think before you speak? Are you an active listener? What does this concept mean to you?
- Do you listen to and learn from negative feedback? Are you able to give negative feedback in a way that others are receptive to?
- How well do you acknowledge others? How well do they acknowledge you? Do you readily give your time to help others?
- Do you have a balanced view of yourself? What are your strengths? What do you enjoy? What are your weaknesses? What are three things you would like to improve about yourself?
- Do you empathize with others? What does "empathizing" with someone mean to you?
- Do you apologize willingly? Are you able to forgive and move forward?
- Do you keep to your commitments? Are you on time? Do you over-commit your time or your abilities?
- How do you practice self-care? List three primary activities that are your go-to for self-care.
- Do you focus on what you can control? Are you okay with things you can't control?

If any of these questions leave you wondering where you stand or make you feel as if you could improve in that area, do not worry. You will have more chances to self-evaluate and improve your EI. For those questions where you answered yes or positively, you are off to a great start and will be able to leverage your current EI to improve as you go.

GET-A-GRIP EMOTIONAL INTELLIGENCE ASSESSMENT ©

Next step... take the assessment in Appendix 1 to establish your initial baseline and have a point to measure for improvement.

After completing and grading the assessment, consider the questions at the beginning of the chapter and how they might apply to you:

- How will continuously cultivating your emotional intelligence contribute to your lifelong personal and professional growth, learning, and development?
- How will you practice emotional intelligence to achieve balance, resilience, and emotional stability in facing challenges?
- What role will your level of emotional intelligence play in building and maintaining healthy, positive relationships with peers, supervisors, subordinates, friends, and family?

Please save your writings for comparison with where you stand when you finish this book to see the growth you will have already experienced and can expect as you continue your journey to improve and develop your EI.

Let's build up your EI skill set and move forward and upward.

Your Life. Your Health. Your Journey... Take Action!

CHAPTER 2
SELF-AWARENESS – YOUR JOURNEY TO SELF-DISCOVERY

"Look outside and you will see yourself. Look inside and you will find yourself."

DREW GERALD

Perhaps the most critical of the 4 Pillars of EI is Pillar 1 – Self-Awareness. The foundation of Pillar 1 helps you build trust, improve relationships, and enhance many soft skills. Self-awareness is categorized as both internal, how you see yourself, and external, how others view you. There are many tools you can use to improve both. This chapter will look at ways to assess your self-awareness and how you can get a grip on your inner self.

Psychologists point out that to discover your true self, you must set the goal for self-discovery. Your central inner force is unique to you as a human being. The discovery of self is a profound source of growth that contributes to healthy development and enhances your overall personal nature.

Self-discovery enhances your abilities, improves your quality of life, and allows you to act effectively on opportunities. Searching for your true self involves a reasonable and intuitive process that is personal and must be done with purpose. When you understand how your unique abilities can impact your purpose-related goals, your actions and reactions to life's situations are significantly enhanced. Your true self lies beneath the surface but is accessible, and discovering it is the first step toward becoming emotionally intelligent.

INTROSPECTION AND SELF-REFLECTION

There are two main reflection processes you can use for introspection—an informal approach and an experimental approach.

- Informal approach—This approach involves examining your thoughts and feelings and reflecting on what they truly mean. You can use the informal approach to focus on a current mental experience or one that has occurred previously.
- Experimental approach—Experimental introspection was first developed by Wilhelm Wundt, "father of experimental psychology", in the mid-1800s. Wundt focused on three core areas of mental functioning: feelings, thoughts, and images. Wundt's findings and revelations back in the 19th century have evolved and developed into today's 21st-century collective field of cognitive psychology (Kim, 2022).

Adopting the informal approach is the most effective way for you to enhance your self-awareness on a daily basis. Reflecting on your emotions and experiences, followed by documenting your insights and discoveries in a diary or journal, presents the simplest path for self-examination over time. Acknowledge the presence of your personal biases and preconceptions. Urge yourself to step beyond your comfort zone's confines for a thorough self-assessment. Opening up to yourself is essential for this method to truly benefit you.

The experimental method regards introspection as an objective and analytical practice, designed to cultivate your ability to self-reflect. This allows you to articulate your sensations, thoughts, experiences, and emotions in response to external stimuli. Through this approach, you're trained to examine your thought processes clinically, distancing yourself from your feelings and emotions. This technique is not particularly effective for individual self-reflection but is more appropriate in a controlled laboratory setting or within professional counseling or therapy sessions facilitated by social workers, psychologists, or psychiatrists.

Importance of Self-Reflection

You learn from your mistakes and experiences along the way, but you only benefit from them when you begin to question their outcome and focus on understanding what needs to change. Self-reflection helps you understand your experience and teaches you how to react to similar situations in the future. You figure out the right behaviors and practices and focus on your strengths. You identify your weaknesses, accept them, and work through them.

You have a subconscious that affects how you view, ponder, and act or react to life around you. Self-reflection makes you aware of your thoughts, brings your subconscious to the surface, and allows you to focus on positives and avoid negatives. You will have a chance to control your emotions and find solutions rather than create more problems.

Techniques for Effective Introspection

There are numerous activities that help us understand self-reflection. Here are a few exercises you can practice for a more in-depth introspection. Use your notebook/journal to record your answers, thoughts, and discoveries.

Self-Examination Exercise 1

Ask yourself: Do I tend to analyze people or provide solutions to their problems without them asking for it?

We often provide information we know is beneficial to us and would like to share it with someone we feel needs it. Have you ever experienced someone doing this to you? While your analysis and solutions may make sense for you, they won't necessarily benefit or make sense for the other person. Be aware that trying to solve others' problems may not be what they seek. Often, you just being a sounding board and listening to what they have to say is all they want and need.

If you sense they want advice, find out for certain that they do want it before giving it. As Stephen Covey's Habit 5 states, "Seek first to understand, then to be understood." Know that your advice is wanted and will be valued before you give it.

Self-Examination Exercise 2

Think of a recent incident in which you became upset because of something another person did or said. Let's examine the problem and find a resolution.

You may have been anxious, angry, sad, or frustrated. Do you think you should confront them and tell them how they upset you? How did they make you feel? Mad, sad, or frustrated? Or should you avoid them or the issue because they get defensive and angry whenever you say something?

Avoid putting others on the defense by taking stock of how an incident affects you and makes you feel, and then explain that to them using "I" messages: "I feel anxious when...", "I get angry when...". This approach ensures you are not blaming those feelings on others. Too often we tell others, "You frustrate me..." or "You made me so mad...", placing the control of our emotions on them.

Reflecting on your recent incident, how would you change the way you handled it as it was happening? What conversation would you have with the other person? Do you feel you would have more control of yourself and the situation through using this approach? How would this make the other person feel?

Getting a grip on your emotional intelligence gives you the self-awareness to own your feelings and the ability to control them yourself instead of being controlled by the actions of others.

Self-Discovery (Real-Life Story)

Self-discovery is all about knowing your capabilities and working on them. Let's look at an example. Theresa Fianko was an unemployed marketing specialist in the Middle East country of Dubai. During this time, she journaled her frustrations, anger, and irritation about the job market. Through these writings, she discovered a passion for writing and changed her direction in life.

With the force and feeling she was putting into her writing, she realized it was something she enjoyed, was very good at, and had excellent career prospects. She took up a diploma course in writing, then went on to build the global platform Diaspora Digital News, an integrated media and marketing social impact broadcasting service.

Benefits of Self-Discovery

Self-discovery is your ability to reflect, explore, and grow from various situations in life and gain a clear sense of purpose and direction. It positively impacts your life, helps you make better decisions, improves relationships, and enhances overall well-being.

Human beings evolve and grow through their life, and being able to discover yourself through this journey can impact the growth and direction your life takes. Here are a few reasons why self-discovery is essential:

Better Values

Self-discovery helps clear your thoughts and think rationally. This clear mindset helps you understand your values and focus on them to make better decisions and take the right action.

What are your top 3 values that direct your life?

Better Decision-Making

When you're able to understand yourself better, you'll be able to make decisions that align with your goals and values.

From the 3 values you listed above, what recent major decisions or actions would you change to better align yourself with your values? How would you change those decisions?

Become Self-Aware

Self-awareness is the foundation of personal growth and development, and understanding yourself is the only way to do this work.

How well do you feel you understand yourself?

Identifying Your Strengths

Self-discovery helps you understand your strengths and how to focus on the right areas in life to succeed.

What are 3 strengths that help lead you to success?

Discover Passion

Self-discovery often helps you identify what you're passionate about. Like Theresa (from the narrative above), it helps you choose your path to success.

What are 3 things that you are passionate about? That you consider a calling? That you were meant to do in life?

Sense of Purpose

Having a purpose in life motivates you and helps steer you in the right direction.

Above, you listed 3 things you are passionate about. What do you see as your purpose for each of them? How might you pursue each of those passions with a heightened sense of purpose?

Identify Your Weaknesses

Self-discovery also helps you identify your weak areas and develop a plan to address and improve them.

What are 3 improvements you would like to make to yourself and your life? How will you accomplish them?

Become Resilient

Resilience is important for moving forward. Get up, dust yourself off, and get going again. You accept the things you cannot change. Self-discovery is important for building resilience.

How do you handle failures? Do you quit and just move on? Or do you learn from them, make changes, and continue to strive for success?

Better Relationships

When you understand how your interactions impact others, it will help you improve your relationship with them.

Pick the most important relationship in your life and list three things you could do to improve it.

Health and Wellness

Self-discovery can enhance your overall health and well-being by giving you focus on better mental health, reduce stress and anxiety, and build self-confidence.

What problems do you face with your mental health? What daily stressors do you face? What causes you anxiety? What, in your life, would you like to feel more confident about?

Self-discovery is a crucial component of better personal growth. Self-awareness is the primary foundation for developing your emotional intelligence. Building your self-awareness becomes the reward once you set out to do it.

- Use your values and passions to direct you.
- Emphasize your strengths and make improvements where needed.
- Seek to understand yourself and your priorities. Take control of your emotions.
- Use failure as a lesson, like an experiment. Learn from it, make changes as needed, and continue forward to build success.

Strategies for Maintaining Self-Awareness

Being self-aware is understanding yourself, whether it's your strengths and weaknesses, decision-making, or the ability to judge others based on behavior. A self-aware person takes responsibility for their actions and accepts the mistakes they make. They are not overly critical and focus on problem-solving to improve the situation. As you grow your self-awareness, you need to nurture what you have and feed it like a living organism. Here are a few strategies to help you nurture, feed, and maintain your self-awareness.

Meditation

Meditation is a powerful technique for becoming more attuned to yourself. The quiet, calm environment helps you concentrate, clear your thoughts, and focus on what matters most. Meditating regularly helps you clear your thought processes of external clutter and builds self-awareness.

Find a quiet place to calm your mind. Meditate for at least 10 minutes, more if you can spare the time. Use soft music or directed meditation recordings to bring focus to you, your body, your breathing, your being. Set an alarm if you need it so you can concentrate inside yourself, not on time, not the world external to you.

Identifying Your Goals

You should have a set of goals that lead you to achieve what you want in life. However, day-to-day responsibilities can get in the way and cause you to drift away from these goals. Have a plan to direct your life so you stay on course to accomplish your goals. Consider your values and go deep into your self-awareness to list your core goals to support these values.

- Line out the steps and actions needed to achieve these core goals.
- Begin the journey one step at a time and track your progress. Make a daily plan for the steps to move toward your core goals.
- Review regularly, such as once a week, to keep focus on your core goals and achieve them efficiently.
- List your day-to-day responsibilities in your daily plan, along with your steps toward your core goals. Make them a part of your plan, not a disrupter. Check off the tasks as you complete them.
- Make it a goal in itself to fulfill your responsibilities and include this goal with your deeper core goals to keep balance direction in your life.

Ask for Feedback

You will use your own reflection and feedback to build upon as you progress toward your goals, but realize it is only the viewpoint of one, you. You will benefit from the observations and opinions of others as well. Seeking the perspective of others will give you a bird's eye view of your actions, how they impact others, and what you might change to improve. Both informal feedback and directed coaching will lead you to success levels that you cannot achieve on your own.

Communicate With Loved Ones

People who are closest to you know you best. They're the ones who've seen you at both your best and your worst. They can give you valuable insight into your strengths and weaknesses, particularly with your awareness of your relationships with them and others. Ask them for feedback to get clear insight into the areas you excel in and where you need to improve.

Maintain a Journal

Writing down your thoughts solidifies them and helps you become and stay self-aware. You can go back and reflect on your entries and evaluate the achievement of your goals. Your journal keeps a record of where you have been and is a living document witnessing your growth and direction in life.

Create an Action Timeline

An action timeline constrains and structures the path you will follow to achieve your goals and increases self-awareness. It will help you understand what matters most, what needs to be done now, and the work you must do to achieve your goals.

Stay True to Yourself

The process of self-awareness may seem like a complex journey. However, it is much simpler when you stay true to yourself. This gives you a direct path without the detours of self-deception.

Acceptance

Accept who you are to achieve self-awareness. Like being true to yourself, deception does not belong here. Whether you're an introvert or extrovert, an optimist or pessimist, conscientious or forgetful, you cannot change your core nature. But you can be aware of it, control your behavior and emotions based on it, and build on your EI accordingly. You must be comfortable with yourself, irrespective of your personality traits.

RECOGNIZING EMOTIONS

Now, let's look at the importance of and ways to recognize your emotions. A simple way to be aware of your emotions is by noticing what you feel. Close your eyes and ask yourself, how are you feeling? Come up with one-word answers to address your feelings. There are no right and wrong answers. Be aware of what you're feeling and find the most obvious one.

There will be moments when your feelings are obvious; other times, they are subtle. You are excited when your team wins. You are sad when your friend gets hurt. You are anxious when stepping out of your comfort zone. You are uncomfortable when talking to your boss. Feelings and emotions are signals your body sends out that will help you or hinder you, depending on your awareness. There are various ways to stay aware of your emotions and work with them, not against them.

Naming Your Feelings

When you begin noticing how you're feeling, it's good to associate a word with that feeling. For example, if you're scared, you can name it "anxiousness," or when you're happy about something going well, you can say you're "proud." Naming feelings helps you notice feelings right away. So, what are you feeling right now? Write it down.

Tracking Emotions

When you name your emotions, you can start tracking them. If you're feeling happy, track how often you feel it during the day and what triggers it. Maybe a friend showing up or calling makes you happy, or maybe eating special treats, like pizza, makes you happy. Note down how strong the feeling is each time you feel it. Track your emotions in your notebook. Make entries two to three entries each day on the emotions you have felt and why. Review at the end of the week for trends or negative situations.

Come Up With New Names

Apart from giving conventional names to your feelings, you can see what other names you can come up with. For example, how many words describe happiness? You can describe this feeling as "delight," "joy," or "excitement." How many words can you think of? Try doing this exercise with different feelings as you track your emotions throughout the week.

Journal About Your Emotions

Take time at the end of each day to note or review your feelings and how often you felt them. You can even compose a poem or a song, or draw or paint something based on your feelings.

Never ignore your feelings. Acknowledge everything you feel during the day. Accept your feelings, and don't judge yourself. Remind yourself that all emotions are normal and that you should make wise choices based on them. If your feelings are overwhelming, make sure you speak with someone about them and possibly seek professional help through counseling or therapy. Complex emotions are part of life; the sooner you accept them, the better your life can be.

Importance of Acknowledging Emotions

As seen above, feelings can become overwhelming. People of all ages struggle when managing their responses to certain feelings. For example, you may do or say something in anger that you regret later or get sad and stay in isolation in your home or room. These are emotions that can be handled, and it is important that you acknowledge your emotions and accept them so that you can understand what you are feeling and deal with them appropriately. Here are a few reasons to understand your emotions better:

- Understanding the reason behind what you're feeling helps you react better. You can know what's happening and why it's happening. For example, you may not understand how your coworkers may affect your mindset, and you may end up taking out the frustration on your family members instead of dealing with the real issue.
- Controlling your emotions is important. Emotions usually affect people's behavior and mood. Whenever you're sad or angry, you may find that you take out the frustration on the people around you. Recognize what triggers these negative emotions so that you can understand the source of them, control your reaction, and deal with the source. Similarly, when children start having negative feelings, they will not feel like playing or participating in activities or hobbies. Like adults, children also need to recognize what triggers negative feelings so they can stay in control of their reactions and not blame others. This behavior will impact their overall life quality.
- Negative thoughts can prevail when you struggle or fail to identify your feelings. Thoughts like *I'm not good enough* or *I can't do that* can creep in when you're not in the right frame of mind. When you start recognizing your feelings,

you can react better. Your thought process does not need to be negative, and you can change your feelings by triggering happier thoughts. Choose to be positive.

When you begin recognizing negative feelings, you can ask for help to clarify or confirm your emotions. If you are unsure of how you are feeling in a relationship, discuss it with those in that relationship with you. A talk with your friend, parent, or spouse may be all the help you need, but professional help is also a consideration. When you don't grant recognition to your feelings, your negative thoughts will cloud your judgment, and you may take drastic steps and burn bridges, or worse, with your actions.

Emotional Triggers and Their Recognition

A trigger is anything that triggers an unexpected or intense emotional response. A trigger could be a person, a situation, a thing, or a place. Triggers are different from threats. While researchers aren't sure why the human brain forms triggers, a realistic justification is that it records a threatening experience and reminds us of it when triggered.

The brain usually connects a fight-or-flight response when it experiences such a trigger. The brain usually reacts as if it's under threat, and this reaction is similar to a Post-Traumatic Stress Disorder (PTSD) symptom.

Triggers usually make you feel like you're reliving the same experience, but how do you know you're responding to a trigger? While triggers usually differ for each person, the symptoms stay the same. Any of the symptoms below indicate you are likely responding to a trigger.

- panicking or getting scared
- profusely sweating or experiencing breathing difficulties
- inexplicable mood changes
- no emotional control
- outbursts of sadness or anger

Emotions and Their Physical Manifestations

While emotions are usually considered non-material, the body also experiences certain symptoms. A classic example is when artists try to depict sadness or anger through a painting. While the emotion is felt in the head, the physical attributes, like droopy eyes and puffed cheeks, tell the story to others.

Your body and your brain provide constant feedback to each other through the mind-body connection. For example, you're more energetic when you're happy, and there's a spring in your step. Similarly, when you're sad, your physical stature will droop, and you will avoid eye contact with others.

Recognizing Emotions (Real-Life Story)

A soldier, John Walters, returned from deployment and was happy to be reunited with his family after almost nine months. He was anxious and on edge from the daily threats and carnage faced in the war zone where his unit deployed. Things went well at home, and John settled down as civilian life took over. It was the 4th of July weekend, and neighbors and friends gathered at John's place to celebrate his homecoming and Independence Day.

All was going well till the fireworks began. A few minutes later, John began sweating profusely. When a string of firecrackers went off, John bailed out of his chair and hid behind his truck. He curled up into a ball, covered his head, and rocked back and forth. He lashed out when his wife and friends tried to help. His wife called 911. An ambulance was dispatched. John was sedated and taken to the local hospital. After several tests and mental health evaluations, John was diagnosed with PTSD.

John began seeing a psychiatrist and slowly opened up about his feelings. The constant threat and chaos found in his deployed assignment in Iraq had taken a toll on his mind, and he wasn't even aware that it had affected him so much. The psychiatrist advised journaling as a tool for John to cope with his PTSD.

Soon, John began sharing his thoughts with his wife and friends through his journal. It made it easier to understand what he was going through. People made an extra effort to avoid triggers for John, which helped him recover faster.

EMOTIONAL AWARENESS TOOLS

Emotions are part of everyone's life. It's important to control difficult emotions, and various tools can help you do so. As mentioned earlier, emotional control starts with acknowledging the emotion. You can then formulate a strategy to get the desired outcome. With better control over your emotional reaction, you can respond more tolerably. This section will look at different tools to help with emotional awareness.

Emotional Journaling

Journaling, as previously mentioned, is an excellent way to express thoughts and make sense of your feelings. Emotionally intelligent individuals use journaling to look at their decisions and see how they could have reacted better. Journalling also helps you identify behavioral patterns and improves self-awareness. This practice comes in handy when you're overwhelmed by emotions and have no one to speak with. You can solidify your emotions on paper. Your journal will help you look at past instances so you can see what helped you.

Meditation and Mindfulness

Meditation and mindfulness, also mentioned previously, allow you to explore your emotions and thoughts without judgment. These skills help you develop even greater emotional intelligence and better understand your emotions.

Assessment Tools

Various emotional and psychological assessment tools help you identify multitudes of different factors that define who you are and how you engage in life and relationships. These tools give insight into your well-being and success paths you will do well pursuing. Examples of these tools include the Myers-Briggs personality profile test and the previously noted BarOn EQi test for emotional quotient and MSCEIT test for EI. The Get-A-Grip Emotional Intelligence Assessment included in the Appendix of this book gives you a good perspective on your EI. These tools use many different dimensions but should not be used as a diagnosis. Links to some assessment tools are included at the end of this chapter and in the Appendix.

Emotional Awareness Apps and Technologies

Various emotional awareness apps can help you better understand your emotions. Self-help therapy, mood trackers, self-care, and brain training apps abound in the smartphone world. These apps teach you what emotions are, how they work, and what you can do to better yourself. Technology has evolved and helps provide an understanding of the factors surrounding us. Just as artificial intelligence proliferates, so do advances in the EI realm.

Benefits of Using Emotional Awareness Tools

Using emotional awareness tools has various benefits. They help you understand yourself better and gain insight into your responses and reactions. As a result, your self-acceptance, understanding, and decision-making will improve. Using these tools also helps you empathize with others' feelings and can strengthen your relationships.

CHAPTER RECAP

This chapter focused on self-awareness and emotional awareness, looking at the journey to self-discovery through introspection and self-reflection, as well as techniques and benefits for gaining and maintaining self-awareness. We discussed techniques and tools for recognizing your emotions and triggers. Tools for further assessment are also provided below at the end of the chapter.

ACTION ITEMS

Hopefully, you are keeping a journal of your thoughts, emotions, and the exercises found in this book. Your entries will provide you with valuable insight and documentation for reflection to fortify your self-awareness pillar.

Write a Letter

As discussed above with journaling, writing is a process that helps you get a clear picture of your emotions. Start by writing a letter to yourself. Focus on a few actions you want your future self to take. Start with simple scheduling/to-do items:

- What is my plan for tomorrow? The coming week?
- When will I complete my work/school assignment?
- What other items need to be done? What day will I do these tasks?

Move on to more personal, introspective actions:

- I am grateful for _____ in my life. I will return/pass on this gratitude by _____.
- One change I would like to work on this week is _____. I will do the following to make this change happen:

    1.
    2.
    3.

- I need to bring about this change in my life because _____.

Handle Everyday Hassles Better

Often, your built-in responses are triggered due to everyday hassles. These hassles could be anything from being stuck in traffic, annoying team members, or arguing with your spouse. Note how you last reacted to these situations and write about what you could have done better. Contemplate and write about how you can manifest a better reaction and how you would like to see it happen the next time.

Share Your Fears

This activity should ideally be done with another person. This other person could be your partner, your coworker, or your sibling. Discuss with them the plan for the exercise and then do the exercise.

Share a doubt or a fear with the other person and then ask them to help you overcome that fear. Their response should be, "I'll help you overcome that fear." In return, they should share their doubt or fear, and you should say the same, "I'll help you overcome that fear." This listening exercise is excellent for both of you and helps you express issues with others.

Journal about your feelings while doing this exercise. As a follow-up, you and the other person can get together a few days later and discuss how you feel now that you have expressed your doubt or fear.

TOOLS FOR FURTHER ASSESSMENT

Get-A-Grip Emotional Intelligence Assessment ©:

> at the end of this book in Appendix 1.

Additional exercises to help you Get A Grip On Your Emotional Intelligence are available to you FREE:

> To get this content, please send me an email at: KennyLeeBooks@gmail.com

* * *

For personality profile (similar to Myers-Briggs), go to: https://www.mypersonality.net/quiz

This 50-question quiz costs $1.99 (at time of publishing) to get your results. Follow-on testing is also available with subscription.

If you wish to test your emotional intelligence beyond your test provided in the Appendix of this book, go to:

   https://thepersonalitylab.org/eq-test

CHAPTER 3
SELF-MANAGEMENT: EMOTIONAL REGULATION AND CONTROL

"You have power over your mind – not outside events. Realize this, and you will find strength."

MARCUS AURELIUS, MEDITATIONS

Josie's morning had spiraled out of control the moment she woke up. The alarm was silent. She had overslept. The sun was glaring into her bedroom, mocking her tardiness. In a frantic rush, she skipped her usual morning rituals, grabbed her bag and purse, then dashed out the door. The drive to the accounting firm where she worked was a blur of honking horns and red traffic lights, each minute ticking by amplifying her growing sense of dread. By the time she arrived, her heart was racing, not just from the run from the parking lot to her desk, but from the overwhelming realization that she was late for work on a crucial day.

As she settled into her chair, trying to catch her breath, she could feel the weight of her boss's gaze from across the room. Was he staring at her? She didn't dare look up. The air in the office felt thick, suffocating, as she attempted to appear composed and dive into her work. The uneasy feeling in her stomach grew as she desperately tried to remember the whereabouts of the project due today—a project she had painstakingly worked on for weeks. She looked for the file in her bag. No, not there. She hadn't printed it yet. It was on her desk computer. No, that file was only the draft. The finalized project was on her laptop. At home. On the kitchen table.

The combination of her boss's constant scrutiny, her lateness, and the missing project pushed Josie into the throes of an anxiety attack. Her breath became short and shallow, her chest tightened, and the room seemed to spin around her. Panic gripped her, rendering her paralyzed in her seat. It was a stark reminder of the invisible struggles she faced, struggles that the rigid environment of the accounting firm did little to accommodate. Why was this happening? Why couldn't she control it? In that moment, surrounded by numbers and deadlines, Josie realized the importance of seeking support and understanding in her battle with anxiety, a battle that extended far beyond the confines of her workplace.

Emotions play a significant role in your life. The anxiety that overwhelms Josie is one of the negative emotions that you may face. Anger, sadness, and depression are other common emotions you may deal with.

Things don't unfold as planned. You are running late for an appointment. The freeway is gridlocked during the morning rush hour. Or you are fighting traffic in a large city. You curse at the truck in front of you. You become irritated with your spouse and child who are with you in the car. You lash out, telling them to shut up, then flip the middle finger at the driver who just cut in front of you. The anger is real; road rage is real. Why does this happen to you? Why can't you control it?

Or unexpected misfortune strikes... You get laid off at work. Or your dog died. Now what? You lie on the couch, Netflix on your 72-inch high-def screen. You stare, not seeing the program, only the gloom ahead. It is sunny out. You have the blackout curtains pulled. Traffic and life honk and hum along outside your apartment building. They do not drown out the negative thoughts in your head or the sadness in your heart. You curl up and close your eyes. Sadness subdues. Depression overwhelms. Just make it go away.

Regardless of the specifics – anxiety, anger, sadness, or depression – your emotions are real. Name them, understand them, and accept them to enable yourself to deal with them. Using self-management and controlling your emotions before, during, and after an incident go hand in hand. This chapter will delve into effective strategies for you, illustrating how mastering your emotions yields more positive outcomes.

THE SCIENCE OF SELF-MANAGEMENT

Emotional control and regulation involve modifying the strength of your emotional responses without suppressing or avoiding your feelings and managing the emotions you feel along with how you express them. Some people have a natural aptitude for emotion regulation. They exhibit high emotional intelligence, being cognizant of their emotions and those of others around them. Even though these people may seem perpetually composed, they also experience negative emotions. Yet, they have coping mechanisms to self-regulate during emotionally taxing situations.

Fortunately, you can learn self-management skills and build them with practice. As you develop the capability to handle negative emotional experiences, you will experience a significant positive impact on your mental and physical well-being.

Consider an everyday-type situational scenario where you're at a friend's birthday party. After the gifts are opened and the cake is enjoyed, everyone gathers to watch a movie. You soon realize that your friend has chosen a horror film. While some guests relish the thrill of scary movies, you find them unsettling and prone to causing nightmares. The room darkens, and a spine-chilling soundtrack starts. You were comfortable and enjoying the party until now. Faced with this situation, what would be your response?

Psychologists recommend considering the following strategies to regulate your emotions for positive results:

- **Opting to exit the environment:** In this scenario, you might decide to leave the room to find out if some of your friends are engaged in games or socializing elsewhere. Often, just being aware that you have the power to change your situation can help alleviate discomfort.
- **Finding a distraction:** Another option is to remain and continue watching the film while finding ways to distract yourself. You could close your eyes during frightening scenes or focus on less intimidating aspects, like the costume design. You might be surprised at how much less fearful you feel by not concentrating on the horror elements.
- **Reframing your perspective:** This approach involves altering your viewpoint of the movie. Continuously remind yourself that the characters are just actors on a set, and try visualizing the behind-the-scenes aspects, like the time it took for the makeup to be applied.

- **Modifying how you express emotions:** By adopting this method, you would continue watching the film but choose to laugh instead of showing fear. This approach helps in not revealing your fear to others around you.

Which one do you think would work for you in this case? Think of instances where you may have used these strategies before. Consider Josie's situation at the beginning of the chapter. How might she use these strategies to handle her anxiety? What about the scenarios regarding anger, sadness, and depression?

These strategies are all part of the psychological science of Cognitive Behavioral Therapy, the principles of which will be discussed more in a few moments. Before going further, let's step away for a moment and look at the biology of emotions.

Biological Basis of Emotions

Emotions are multifaceted and deeply personal experiences that integrate feelings, thoughts, physical changes, and actions, often accompanied by alterations in the nervous system and observable in facial expressions.

Among the numerous theories exploring the essence and function of emotions, the evolutionary theory proposed by Charles Darwin in the 1870s stands out. This theory posits that emotions have developed over time because they provide survival benefits. For example, the emotion of fear evolved to prompt actions enhancing survival chances. Darwin suggested that emotional expressions, particularly facial ones, are inherent and crucial for rapidly discerning someone's intentions or threat level.

Modern interpretations of the evolutionary perspective on emotions continue to underscore the significance of inborn responses to stimuli. These perspectives regard emotions as evolutionary tools and focus less on the roles of cognition and learning, although they recognize that these factors can influence emotional experiences.

These theories propose that certain primary emotions are universal across cultures, such as happiness, surprise, contempt, anger, disgust, sadness, and fear. Other emotions are considered to be variations or combinations of these core emotions. For example, terror is viewed as a heightened form of the primary emotion, fear.

How Emotions Are Formed in the Brain

Emotional experiences involve the activation of various nervous system components, including the brain and the autonomic nervous system.

Four structures in the brain play vital roles in producing, processing, and managing emotions:

- The hypothalamus functions as the executor of emotions, managing the physical and behavioral responses linked to different feelings.
- The amygdala, known as the emotion orchestrator, plays a critical role in recognizing and interpreting emotional cues, particularly those related to fear and threats.
- The striatum is involved in habit formation and addictive behaviors, contributing to the reward and reinforcement aspects of emotions.
- The prefrontal cortex assesses the suitability of emotional responses based on the situation. It influences and

regulates the amygdala and striatum, thus shaping our emotional reactions.

Your emotions are, therefore, a product of these complex and interconnected neural processes.

Your control, your grip on your emotional intelligence, is through the conditioning and use of the prefrontal cortex to influence and regulate the amygdala and striatum.

Emotions are often analyzed in terms of two key aspects: valence and intensity. Valence describes whether an emotion is positive or negative and ranges from avoidance to approach tendencies. Intensity, meanwhile, refers to the strength and level of arousal of an emotion. This framework, though simplified, is helpful in associating facial expressions with the brain mechanisms responsible for them, even though it might not fully encompass the nuances of every emotion.

Impact of Hormones on Emotions

Hormones, acting as chemical messengers, are released by glands into the bloodstream and play a pivotal role in regulating various bodily functions and emotions.

Some of these hormones are known as "feel-good hormones" due to the positive and, at times, euphoric feelings they induce. These hormones, which include serotonin, dopamine, endorphins, and oxytocin, influence your mood but also act as neurotransmitters, facilitating communication between nerve cells.

Natural methods exist to increase the levels of these hormones. Lifestyle modifications like dietary changes, regular physical activity, and meditation practices can potentially enhance our mood.

While quick solutions like supplements might seem appealing for mood enhancement or depression prevention, they are often unnecessary for most people and can sometimes lead to unwanted or even severe side effects. For example, supplements like 5-hydroxytryptophan (5-HTP), intended to boost serotonin levels, have been associated with risks like liver and brain damage and a rare but serious condition called eosinophilia-myalgia syndrome (EMS), impacting muscles, skin, and lungs.

You should consult a healthcare professional before starting any supplements. They can determine if the supplement is appropriate and safe for you. You may not need supplements unless there's a specific hormone deficiency. In cases where a condition involves abnormally low hormone levels, such as thyroid deficiency or adrenal insufficiency, your doctor can prescribe suitable medication for management.

The Role of Neurotransmitters

The significance of neurotransmitter levels in the brain in relation to the onset of specific emotions is well-established. Neurotransmitters, which are crucial in regulating a range of mental and physical processes including perception, cognition, and consciousness, also significantly influence our emotions and behaviors. The interplay and relative concentrations of these neurotransmitters in our brain are key factors in determining our emotional well-being.

There are three main neurotransmitters, each linked to specific emotional states. The variety of emotions we experience is a result of the different combinations of these neurotransmitters. Each neurotransmitter corresponds to particular emotions as follows:

- **Serotonin:** Serotonin is linked to feelings of punishment, dislike, and sadness.
- **Dopamine:** Dopamine is associated with pleasure, rewards, and feelings of joy.
- **Adrenaline and noradrenaline:** These neurotransmitters are responsible for surprise, arousal, and emotions like fear or anger.

The specific emotional responses influenced by these neurotransmitters are also shaped by various brain regions and the functioning of their receptors. In essence, the combination of neurotransmitter activity, their concentrations, and the brain's role collectively form the basis of our emotional experiences.

Relationship Between Emotions and Physical Health

When negative emotions arise from excessive rumination on past events or ongoing anxiety rather than a response to present circumstances, they can lead to various health issues. Frequent negative emotions and tendencies toward aggression, hostility, or anger, are linked to several physical health problems, including heart disease and high blood pressure.

Depressive moods also notably affect cellular immunity, which intensifies with the severity and duration of the depression. This impact manifests in several ways, such as a reduced response of lymphocytes to antigens, lower activity of natural killer (NK) cells, and an overall decrease in white blood cells.

On the flip side, a positive outlook on life brings numerous health advantages. These include lowered blood pressure, decreased risk of heart issues, improved weight management, stable blood sugar levels, and greater longevity. The benefits of a positive mindset extend beyond mental well-being to influence brain health, neural functioning, immune response, cardiovascular health, and hormonal balance, all of which help the body manage stress effectively.

MASTERING SELF-MANAGEMENT AND EMOTIONAL REGULATION

Cultivating effective emotional regulation strategies is key to developing coping skills, self-management, and sustaining emotional health. It is crucial to discern which strategies are beneficial and which maladaptive behaviors should be avoided.

Cognitive Behavioral Therapy (CBT) has been proven most successful in developing emotional regulation and self-management. CBT may be combined with other talk therapy and medications for some dysfunctional issues, but CBT, by far, yields the best and quickest results of the three. It is goal-oriented, so treatment only lasts until your goal is achieved. CBT is action-based; you take action, you get results. It is a well-researched method of therapy that supports you at your own pace. Once you achieve your goal, you can move on to more improvement in the same area or set new objectives and goals in another area you would like to work on.

The five fundamental action steps you take in Cognitive Behavioral Therapy are:

1. **Make A List.** List the thoughts and associated behaviors you wish to modify. Pick one area to focus on.
2. **Record Unproductive Thoughts**. When you have these unproductive thoughts or exhibit undesired behaviors, make note of what, when, and where they occurred.
3. **Create Replacement Thoughts.** From your list of unproductive thoughts, develop opposing, positive thoughts that you will use to replace them for a better

outcome. Select a positive image to visualize each time you make the replacement.
4. **Read Your List Often.** Develop a habit through repetition. Read often to reinforce.
5. **Notice And Replace.** Notice when the unproductive thoughts arise and replace them with your productive, positive thoughts and visualization. Continue to develop as a habit.

One of the great things about these CBT fundamentals is that you can practice them outside of the clinical therapy arena. Putting the principles to work for you under your own plan of action fortifies both Pillar 1 and Pillar 2 of your EI foundation… so that you can get a grip on your emotional intelligence.

Psychologists have identified six emotion-regulation strategies: acceptance, avoidance, problem-solving, reappraisal, rumination, and suppression. In the short term, all strategies may have viable applications in handling your emotions. You may need to suppress or avoid your emotions in an emergency to handle the situation effectively. Thinking deeply and thoughtfully about your emotions for short periods allows you to analyze them more fully.

But in the long term, acceptance, reappraisal (altering your thoughts or perceptions about a situation to change your emotional response), and problem-solving are the three healthy options. Avoidance and suppression involve hiding or restraining emotional expression and lead to negative outcomes like dissatisfaction and poor well-being. Chronic rumination – compulsively focusing on your own negative thoughts – will likewise have negative effects on mental and physical health.

Seeking answers here in this book shows that you have accepted the issues, are reappraising your emotional responses, and are seeking to solve the problems your emotional responses are causing. You are already implementing self-management to better yourself. Congratulations! You are already halfway to the solution.

For more specific information on the management of anxiety, anger, sadness, and depression, please see Appendix 2.

As part of self-awareness, you must accept the emotions you are experiencing. You strive to regulate your emotional responses – dial them up or down – as you work on your self-management and progress toward self-mastery. There are three main avenues to regulate and modulate your negative emotions:

- **Reduce the triggers of the emotion:** You can avoid triggers or still experience a trigger event without an unwanted surge in negative emotions.
- **Reduce the emotion's intensity:** Once the negative emotion is triggered, you can regulate the intensity to avoid being overwhelmed and keep yourself in a manageable state of emotional response.
- **Reduce the emotion's duration:** You can reduce the peak duration of the emotion and also return more quickly to your baseline emotional state.

You have learned your emotional regulation skills in life as part of normal development into adulthood. Some factors and experiences do have negative impacts on this development. Trauma, emotional invalidation or abuse, and genetic/biological sensitivities can all have a negative, dysfunctional influence on your ability to regulate your emotions.

Skill sets that will help with self-management are:

- **Mindfulness:** Identify your emotions before they get out of control and exercise cognitive control strategies so you don't fixate on what overwhelms you.
- **Distress tolerance:** Accept and work with what is unpleasant instead of avoidance and denial of negative urges and emotions.
- **Emotional regulation:** Reduce your susceptibility to negative emotions and their intensity and duration, as discussed above.
- **Interpersonal effectiveness:** Change your environment and those around you to reduce the intensity of your experiences.
- **Practicing positive self-talk:** It's important to avoid negative self-talk in moments of overwhelming emotions. Adopting a self-compassionate and empathetic approach can transform negative thoughts into positive affirmations, helping to lessen the impact of challenging emotions.

By implementing these strategies, individuals can enhance their ability to regulate and manage their emotions. This practice, in turn, can contribute to improved overall emotional well-being and resilience in challenging situations.

Importance of Emotional Control

Difficulty in managing emotions is a common issue. However, for some, emotions can be consistently overpowering, leading to unhealthy coping mechanisms like substance misuse or self-injury.

Emotional dysregulation occurs when emotions or events are interpreted in a way that causes overwhelming distress. These interpretations may not reflect the actual situation but can still trigger intense emotional reactions.

As emotions escalate, they become harder to control. To escape these feelings, individuals often engage in negative or self-destructive behaviors, gaining only temporary escape or distraction from the overwhelming emotions. This creates a cycle of dependence on these harmful coping strategies.

Breaking this cycle requires conscious self-regulation efforts, including challenging distorted perceptions, aligning them with reality, and adopting healthier coping methods. This may require professional counseling to get consistent feedback, realignment, and coaching to stay on track. Alone, you can still apply measures and develop healthy habits to make this happen. Your effective self-management strategies can help break the cycle of dysregulation and lead to more constructive emotion management and self-mastery.

Approaches to Handling Negative Emotions

Reflecting on situations that cause stress and negative emotions is crucial for emotional health. Analyzing the sources of these emotions and your reactions can give you valuable insights.

Negative emotions often stem from specific events or circumstances. For example, a heavy workload can be a major stressor. However, it's not just the event but also your interpretation of it that determines your emotional response.

Understanding your emotions and their causes allows you to take steps to address them. This may involve reducing stress triggers, such as delegating tasks or employing time management techniques to balance your responsibilities.

By identifying and addressing stressors and negative emotions, you can move towards a more positive emotional state. This process of introspection and proactive action empowers you to take charge of your emotional well-being.

Positive Emotional Reorientation

Developing a daily gratitude practice is scientifically proven to have a significant positive impact on your life and your outlook for the future. Taking a few minutes each day to reflect and list three to five things that you are grateful for can be transformative. Write these in your journal to solidify their effect. These expressions of gratitude can be as simple as appreciation for a restful night's sleep, a delicious home-cooked meal, or a comforting cup of coffee. The goal of this exercise is to bring attention to the many good things in your life and shift the focus from negative thoughts.

However, while gratitude exercises are helpful in coping with these negative emotions, addressing their root cause is equally important. This may involve delving into deeper issues contributing to these feelings. Take the root cause and negate its significance with your "Attitude of Gratitude" while you address the problem and work to eliminate it completely.

By cultivating a routine of gratitude and introspection, you can develop an arsenal of tools for effectively managing these difficult emotions.

Emotional Control in Stressful Situations

Maintaining calm in emotionally charged conversations can be challenging, often triggering a 'fight or flight' response. However, you can learn and develop control over your physical, psychological, and emotional responses to these situations. Some strategies to manage your reactions include:

1. **Focus on your breathing:** Using your breath as an anchor during difficult conversations helps maintain focus and reduce your panic symptoms. Pay attention to how you breathe while noticing the sensation of air entering and exiting your lungs. Inhaling for a count of two and exhaling for a count of six is an example of a mindfulness technique that diverts panic symptoms away and promotes focus.
2. **Focus on your body:** Remaining still, non-moving, during a difficult conversation can lead to emotions building up rather than dissipating. Experts encourage standing up and walking around, which helps activate the thinking part of your brain and create space, providing perspective and clarity. If standing is not practical, you might try using anchoring, where you cross your fingers or place your feet firmly on the ground, noticing how the floor feels beneath your shoes. Anchoring works in stressful situations as it helps you to re-ground to the present moment.

DEVELOPING EMOTIONAL RESILIENCE

Cultivating emotional resilience is essential for handling life's hurdles and adapting to stressful scenarios. Resilience isn't about dodging or eradicating stress but rather about developing the ability to confront difficulties and bounce back from setbacks. Here are a few approaches to enhance your resilience:

1. **Establish boundaries and be assertive.** Learning to refuse unreasonable demands and safeguarding your time and energy are crucial aspects of building resilience. Hone your skills in self-advocacy, such as requesting what you need and setting clear boundaries.
2. **Embrace acceptance.** Recognizing that stress, discomfort, and change are inevitable parts of life is a key step in fostering resilience. Understand that your thoughts, emotions, and experiences are legitimate and that you can endure by taking proper care of yourself. Reflecting on what aspects of your life you can and cannot control can be enlightening.
3. **Cultivate connections.** Forming strong, supportive bonds with friends, family, or a therapist is a cornerstone of emotional resilience. Being open to seeking and receiving necessary support can provide perspective and enhance your mood.
4. **Seek balance.** Striking a healthy balance between work, relaxation, and leisure activities is vital for sustaining emotional resilience. Make your well-being a priority and plan for activities that bring you happiness. Establishing a routine and dedicating time to self-care are important practices to remain anchored during tough periods.

Impact of Resilience on Overall Well-Being

Resilience plays a crucial role in your ability to navigate and overcome hardships in life. It is the capacity to bounce back and recover from difficult situations, allowing you to adapt and grow in the face of adversity.

Without resilience, you may find yourself easily overwhelmed and struggle to cope with life's challenges, often resorting to unhealthy coping mechanisms such as avoidance, substance abuse, or denial.

As a resilient individual, on the other hand, you will possess the skills and mindset necessary to face adversity head-on. You will be able to draw upon your inner strengths and utilize your support systems to effectively handle difficult situations. This process may involve seeking guidance from your trusted friends, family, or professionals, relying on their problem-solving abilities, or learning new coping strategies that promote growth and well-being.

Resilient people understand that setbacks and hardships are a natural part of life. Rather than being paralyzed by the difficulties you encounter, you will view challenges as opportunities for learning and personal development. By embracing your resilience, you can approach problems with a proactive and solution-oriented mindset, finding ways to navigate obstacles and find meaningful solutions.

Developing resilience is an ongoing process you can cultivate through self-reflection, personal growth, and the development of coping skills. You will learn to regulate emotions, build a positive mindset, and foster healthy relationships and support networks. By strengthening your resilience, we can better manage stress, persevere through difficult times, and emerge stronger and more capable on the other side.

Anecdotes on Developing Emotional Resilience

Erik Weihenmayer, likening himself to an alchemist, has dedicated his life to transforming adversity into triumph. Instead of working with chemical compounds, he focuses on turning proverbial lead into gold through his unwavering determination and resilience.

Growing up as a vibrant and athletic child, Weihenmayer participated in a wide range of activities and developed a passion for wrestling during his early teenage years. However, his trajectory took an unexpected turn when he began losing his sight at the age of 14 due to a progressive disease known as retinoschisis. By the time he graduated from high school, he had become completely blind.

Rather than allowing his blindness to define him or hold him back, Weihenmayer employed his other senses to intensify his experience of the world. Demonstrating incredible perseverance, he even represented his school in the state wrestling competition.

Seeking out new challenges that engaged his sense of touch, Weihenmayer discovered the world of rock climbing. Through the tactility of the sport, he learned to scan for hands and footholds, enabling him to conquer vertical heights that most would deem impossible for a blind person.

Driven by an adventurous spirit and an unyielding belief in his abilities, Weihenmayer went on to achieve extraordinary feats. His crowning accomplishment was ascending Mount Everest, making him the first blind individual to accomplish this remarkable feat. He did not stop there, though. Weihenmayer embarked on numerous other physical endeavors and founded the "No Barriers" movement to inspire and empower others facing life's challenges, demonstrating that they, too, can triumph over adversity.

At the core of Weihenmayer's outlook on life is the guiding motto of the No Barriers: "What's Within You Is Stronger Than What's In Your Way." With this mantra, he exemplifies his approach to life, choosing to harness his internal strength and fortitude to overcome the obstacles that inevitably arise.

While many might view Weihenmayer's journey as extraordinary and admire his bravery, it is undeniable that his resilience and unwavering commitment to keep fighting against all odds are extraordinary traits. Though most people may not face the same extreme circumstances as he has, Erik's story serves as a potent reminder of the remarkable human potential to overcome adversity and thrive.

CHAPTER RECAP

By understanding how to manage our emotions effectively, we can improve our overall well-being and build emotional resilience. Here are a few strategies to help you continue building your emotional resilience.

One strategy is to take a minute each day to focus on your breath. Deep breathing exercises can be incredibly helpful in managing stress and anxiety. Find a quiet space and inhale slowly and deeply through your nose, allowing your lungs to inflate fully. Then, exhale just as slowly through your mouth, emptying your lungs completely. This simple practice can have both immediate and long-term benefits for managing emotions.

ACTION ITEMS

Pick undesired thoughts or behaviors in an area or situation you wish to modify. Use the five action steps of cognitive behavioral therapy to change those thoughts and behaviors to be positive and productive for you:

- List the thoughts or behaviors
- Record the unproductive thoughts
- Create replacement thoughts
- Read your list often
- Notice and replace

Here are two activities to help you continue building your emotional resilience:

- **Keep a gratitude journal.** Gratitude has been shown to have a positive impact on mental health and can help shift our focus to the positive aspects of our lives. Take a few minutes each day to jot down three things you enjoyed and were grateful for during the day. These can be small things, such as a delicious snack, spending time with a beloved pet, or appreciating something beautiful in nature. By cultivating a mindset of gratitude, you can increase your emotional resilience and overall well-being. You can make these entries in your notebook/journal you are using with this book if you wish.
- **Be mindful and deliberate in your digital device usage and news intake.** In our constantly connected world, it can be easy to become overwhelmed by the constant stream of information and the demands of technology. Too much screen time can lead to screen fatigue and emotional exhaustion. Take the time to balance your device usage

with activities that bring you joy and relaxation. Engage in outdoor activities with your family, such as bike rides or nature walks. Rediscover the joys of old-school ways of finding fun and pleasure, whether writing letters, playing board games, or engaging in creative hobbies. Finding this balance can reduce your stress and enhance your emotional well-being.

By incorporating these strategies into your daily routine, you can enhance your emotional resilience and be better equipped to manage your emotions. Remember that building emotional resilience is an ongoing process, so be patient with yourself and continue to prioritize self-care and emotional well-being. The next chapter will discuss empathy's importance and why understanding others is crucial.

MAKE A DIFFERENCE WITH YOUR REVIEW

Unlock the Power of Generosity

"You can't live a perfect day without doing something for someone who will never be able to repay you."

DEBBIE MACOMBER

Hey there, Superstars!

Guess what? People who help others without looking for anything in return are the happiest and coolest people on the playground. And if there's a chance to be one of those happy, cool people, we should totally go for it!

So, I've got a super important question for you...

Would you be willing to help someone you've never met, just because it's a nice thing to do?

Think of someone a bit like you, maybe a little less sure about how to handle their feelings or make good choices. They're looking for a little guidance, just like you might have been.

We're on a mission to make understanding our feelings (that's Emotional Intelligence for you!) something everyone can get better at. Everything we do is to help reach that goal. But, to really make it happen, we need to get the word out to everyone, everywhere.

This is where you come in, my friend. Most people decide which books to read based on what others say about them. So, on behalf of a friend you haven't met yet:

Please help out by leaving a review of this book.

This special favor doesn't cost a dime and takes less than a minute, but it could make someone's day, week, or even change their life. Your review could help...

- ...someone else feel better about themselves.
- ...a friend figure out a tough problem.
- ...a classmate make a new friend.
- ...someone be kinder to themselves and others.
- ...a dream come true for someone out there.

To share a little kindness and make a big difference, all you need to do is leave a review. It's super easy!

Just click on the link below or scan the QR code here:

[https://www.amazon.com/review/review-your-purchases/?asin=B0CZ7V6QCD]

If the idea of helping out someone you've never met makes you smile, you're awesome. Welcome to the club!

I'm super excited to keep sharing fun and helpful tips with you. You're going to love what's coming up next.

Big thanks and high fives,

Your Life. Your Health. Your Journey... Take Action!

~ Kenny Lee

P.S. – Did you know? When you help someone else, it makes them think you're super cool. If you think this book could help someone, why not share it with them?

CHAPTER 4
SOCIAL AWARENESS: EMPATHY, COMPASSION, AND UNDERSTANDING OTHERS

Humans may not boast the physical capabilities to be deemed the fastest, strongest, or largest among animals, but we stand out for our aptitude in comprehension and connection. Our exceptional interpersonal abilities are driven by empathy and the innate propensity to connect and resonate with others' emotions. This trait is fundamental to human behavior and traditionally seen as an inherent aspect of our nature.

Empathy is crucial for our interpersonal connections and societal interactions. It deepens our ability to relate with others, fostering compassion, understanding, and collaboration. Empathy aids in conflict resolution by acknowledging diverse perspectives, leading to balanced and informed decisions. It also drives us to acts of kindness and support for the underprivileged, pivotal in addressing social justice issues and encouraging societal progress.

Recent research, however, points to a decline in empathy in modern society, sparking concerns about its impact on personal relationships, community unity, and societal principles. It becomes imperative to prioritize developing empathy in our daily personal and professional lives. Through practices like active listening, trying to comprehend others' experiences, and engaging in compassionate actions, we can nurture empathy within ourselves and contribute to a more empathetic, compassionate society.

THE ESSENCE OF EMPATHY

Empathy plays a crucial role in enhancing your life. It not only fortifies your connections with others but also ensures that people feel listened to and comprehended. This mutual understanding encourages them to empathize with you in return, enriching your relationships and fostering the sense of belonging we all seek.

Additionally, empathy can:

- **Drive altruistic actions.** It can inspire you to engage in behaviors that positively impact others, such as charitable donations, supporting a friend in need, or offering a comforting embrace.
- **Influence decision-making.** Empathy allows you to assess social situations more accurately, enabling you to act considerately. For instance, recognizing a partner's work-related stress might prompt you to avoid adding more to their plate.
- **Minimize burnout.** Research suggests that empathy can alleviate burnout by fostering smoother communication and teamwork, even in challenging professional settings.
- **Resolve conflicts.** When facing disagreements, empathizing with the other party can prevent harsh criticism or unnecessary harshness. Understanding their viewpoint makes it easier to seek common ground or compromise.

Studies indicate that individuals with robust social networks often experience greater happiness. Since empathy improves interpersonal relationships, it's a vital ingredient for a fulfilling life.

Types of Empathy

Psychologists Paul Ekman and Daniel Goleman have delineated three forms of empathy: Cognitive, Emotional, and Compassionate. By incorporating these distinct types into our interactions, you can forge deeper bonds and cultivate trust with others.

Cognitive empathy is the ability to comprehend and acknowledge another's feelings or thoughts. Often described as "perspective-taking," it's instrumental in understanding someone's circumstances. However, it might sometimes result in a detached connection rather than an authentic emotional bond.

Emotional empathy, on the other hand, is about feeling the emotions of others as if they were our own. It involves a physical and emotional sharing of experiences, to the extent of experiencing sympathetic physical reactions, like cringing at another's pain. This empathy type fosters a deeper, more authentic emotional connection.

Compassionate empathy represents a blend of cognitive and emotional empathy, driving us to take action for someone else's benefit. This empathy type not only allows us to grasp and resonate with another's emotions but also compels us to offer help when necessary. It is a balanced approach that helps in providing effective support without being overwhelmed by emotions or hastily jumping to solutions.

Mastering the balance and application of these three empathy types can lead you to richer, more profound relationships. Empathy enhances our ability to understand and meet the needs of those around us, fostering greater trust and mutual support.

Empathy versus Sympathy

The distinction between sympathy and empathy can be explained in this way: sympathy involves sharing the same emotions as someone else, while empathy means understanding another's emotions without necessarily experiencing them yourself.

Sympathy enables you to connect with another's feelings deeply. For instance, if a friend is sad, showing sympathy means you also feel sad with them, resonating with their emotional state at a profound level. Sympathy occurs organically when you have a deep connection with someone already in place, with family, loved ones, and others close to you.

Conversely, empathy is about recognizing and comprehending someone else's emotions without necessarily mirroring those feelings. It's about mentally placing yourself in another's situation, understanding their emotional viewpoint. Empathy allows you to acknowledge and validate another's feelings, even if they are not emotions you are personally experiencing.

To illustrate this difference, imagine a loved one loses their job. Exercising sympathy would mean feeling the same sadness, disappointment, and frustration they are going through, sharing their emotional burden. In contrast, empathy would involve grasping the range of emotions they might be facing without necessarily experiencing those emotions yourself. With empathy, you provide support and understanding while maintaining a distinct emotional state.

Empathy is appropriate in your professional life—with superiors, subordinates, and coworkers—as well as in your personal connections with those same family members, loved ones, and close friends with whom you share sympathy. Empathy toward acquaintances and even strangers is not only appropriate but also life-enhancing for all involved.

Does Your Empathy Need Some Work?

Empathy is not a binary trait; it exists on a spectrum, with some individuals exhibiting a high capacity for it, while others display much less.

If you possess low empathy, you might feel detached or unconcerned with the suffering of others. In response to a friend's auto accident, you might feel or say, "If you had been more careful..." Or you blame a family member's financial hardship on their lack of effort or laziness. You may think yourself immune to these same misfortunes.

Lack of empathy might also cause you to perceive others as overly sensitive. You might be surprised that your jokes offend your friends. You are oblivious to the hurt caused by your remarks and actions, leading to conflict and misunderstandings.

You show impatience towards those in distress, "Get over it" is your patented response, yet you harbor resentment and are unforgiving of other people's mistakes. You don't truly listen to people's perspectives or consider their feelings and viewpoints.

If you lack empathy, you will never come near your full potential in either your personal or professional life.

But your empathy is not a fixed characteristic, it is like a muscle that can be built up with exercise. By enhancing your ability to listen attentively, observing non-verbal cues, and boosting your emotional intelligence, you can significantly improve your empathetic understanding. Additionally, acknowledging your vulnerability and considering different viewpoints can further cultivate your empathic capacities (Smith, 2023).

EXERCISE YOUR EMPATHY

Learn Listening Skills – Truly empathizing with someone is impossible without genuinely listening to them. Effective listening involves more than just hearing words; it requires deep engagement to comprehend another's circumstances, beliefs, and feelings fully.

To enhance your listening, identify and eliminate any obstacles. Stress, for example, can distract you from fully engaging with another's words. Address any immediate stressors, such as pressing deadlines or physical discomfort, before engaging in conversation. Additionally, avoid multitasking. Put aside your phone and halt other activities to offer your full attention, particularly during sensitive discussions or disagreements (Smith, 2023).

- **Avoid interruptions.** Cutting someone off not only disrupts their thought process but also increases the likelihood of misinterpreting their message. Planning your response while the other person is speaking means you're not fully listening.
- **Suspend judgment.** Entering a conversation with preconceived disagreements can lead you to mentally dismiss the other's points. Listening openly without

immediate criticism or blame encourages a genuine understanding of the speaker's perspective.
- **Show you're listening.** Use non-verbal signals like eye contact and nodding, along with verbal affirmations like "uh-huh," to convey your engagement. These cues encourage the speaker to continue, signaling your interest and care.
- **Seek clarification when needed.** If there's any chance you've misunderstood, ask clarifying questions. This allows the speaker to elaborate, ensuring accurate comprehension and demonstrating your commitment to understanding their viewpoint fully.

Learn and Read Body Language – Effective listening involves more than just absorbing spoken words; it also requires the interpretation of the emotional states conveyed through nonverbal signals. Mastery of body language is crucial in a wide array of social interactions.

Take, for example, a friend who insists they are "doing OK," yet their despondent facial expression suggests otherwise. Or consider how the degree of eye contact on a date might provide insights into the other person's interest levels.

Non-verbal communication includes:

- **Facial Expressions**: These can mirror emotions, ranging from joy to sadness, through various expressions like smiles or frowns.
- **Eye Contact**: The focus and intensity of a person's gaze can indicate their attention or reveal emotions like enthusiasm or weariness.

- **Vocal Tone**: The way someone speaks, including their tone and speech rate, can hint at whether they are joking, serious, confident, or anxious.
- **Body Posture**: The way someone holds their shoulders, either tense or relaxed, can signal feelings of anxiety or ease, respectively.
- **Hand Gestures**: The use or absence of hand movements can express a spectrum of emotions, from nervousness to openness, with the energy of the gestures suggesting excitement or aggression.

Understanding body language is nuanced, as identical gestures can mean different things in various contexts. A person tapping their fingers, for instance, could be a sign of restlessness or simply enjoying the background music.

Key considerations in reading body language include:

- **Consistency**: Ensure nonverbal cues align with verbal messages for greater clarity. Discrepancies may require a deeper exploration of the individual's emotional state.
- **Context**: Focus not solely on a single gesture but on the collective cues to avoid misunderstandings. A comprehensive view of these signals provides a clearer understanding of the individual's feelings.

Remember to be aware of your body language. It communicates volumes to those around you. Postures that suggest closure (crossing your arms) or distraction (looking away) might be perceived as a lack of interest. Promoting interaction through positive body language, such as engaging eye contact or a welcoming smile, is crucial. Additionally, managing stress can aid in reducing inadvertent negative signals, thereby ensuring your body language projects approachability and attentiveness (Smith, 2023).

Be Vulnerable – Embracing empathy involves exposing your vulnerability. Shielding yourself with indifference can alienate you from others, preventing them from trusting or understanding you and limiting your capacity to fully grasp the breadth of their emotions. Here are strategies for becoming more open:

- **Reconsider your view of vulnerability.** It's possible you've been conditioned to see it as a weakness. Yet, revealing your true self to others—allowing them to see and accept you, warts and all—is an act of bravery.
- **Express yourself.** Share your genuine feelings with those close to you. This necessitates introspection and a commitment to transparency. Be ready to acknowledge and share complex emotions like shame, envy, and sorrow. The more you discuss your feelings, the easier it becomes, and you'll find others more inclined to reciprocate.
- **Communicate your needs.** Regularly articulate what you require, whether it's a sympathetic ear or tangible assistance. Speaking up is far healthier than silently struggling. It eases your burdens and makes your loved ones feel valued and necessary.
- **Start gradually.** If discussing your feelings or asking for help feels daunting, begin with small steps. Share everyday frustrations or joys with a friend. Or, make a simple request to your partner, such as going for a stress-relieving walk together.

Let go of concern for your image or striving for perfection. Worrying too much about how you're perceived can lead you to conceal your true self behind a facade of strength and indifference.

Release these inhibitions and accept your flaws. Authenticity fosters deeper connections with those who truly matter (Smith, 2023).

Investigate Other Perspectives – You tend to empathize more readily with those who share your appearance, behaviors, goals, or challenges. This natural inclination, however, can lead to empathy biases based on differences in race, religion, or culture. To overcome these biases, consider the following strategies:

- **Seek out diverse perspectives.** For example, if you're a city dweller, immerse yourself in rural settings; if an atheist, consider attending a religious service; or if politically conservative, listen to liberal viewpoints. Put yourself in the other person's shoes. You don't have to agree; recognizing and respecting differences is crucial too. Open-minded listening can broaden your understanding and appreciation for the richness of diverse human experiences.
- **Delve into fiction.** Immersing yourself in the lives of fictional characters can also foster empathy. Whether through reading novels, watching films, or engaging with other narrative forms, you learn to navigate the inner worlds of characters from various backgrounds. This not only hones your empathetic skills but also encourages you to explore works by creators from diverse cultures, enhancing your understanding and appreciation of their experiences.
- **Challenge your preconceptions.** Interacting with people from varied backgrounds often reveals the inaccuracies in your initial perceptions. Embrace these moments as opportunities for growth, allowing you to reconsider your assumptions in everyday scenarios. This could mean

giving someone the benefit of the doubt for their actions or considering the unseen pressures others may face. Adopting a "what-if" mindset encourages empathy by contemplating alternative explanations for people's behavior.

Remember, enhancing your empathy not only enriches your social experiences and personal happiness but also benefits those around you. Empathy creates a chain reaction, providing emotional support to others and potentially fostering a more understanding and compassionate community (Smith, 2023).

COMPASSION IN ACTION

Integrating compassion into your daily life not only positively impacts others but also boosts your own sense of happiness. While many aim to be compassionate, the pressures of busy schedules often make it challenging to express kindness in everyday interactions.

Yet, it's important to realize that small, simple gestures can significantly uplift someone's day and enhance connections with others. Everyone, no matter how busy, can find moments to incorporate these compassionate acts into their routine. Notice the transformative impact these small kindnesses have on your life.

Simone Weil, a notable French philosopher and social activist, once said, "Attention is the rarest and purest form of generosity." In our fast-paced world, filled with tasks and technological distractions, we often forget the importance of giving someone our full attention. Challenge yourself to be fully present and attentive in your interactions today and observe the positive effects of empathetic listening.

Consider whether your friends and family truly know your appreciation for them. A simple message or phone call expressing gratitude can bring joy and reinforce your relationships. These gestures of recognition can have a lasting impact.

Disconnect from the digital realm occasionally by going offline and engaging with your immediate environment. In doing so, you might find opportunities to make a positive difference. Small actions, like holding a door open for someone or buying a coffee for a person in need, can create a chain of kindness and empathy.

Understand that everyone faces challenges and might sometimes behave in less-than-ideal ways. If someone is late, your boss is short-tempered, or your partner seems distant, respond with empathy rather than irritation. Recognize the possible reasons behind their behavior and react with patience and understanding.

Finally, extend your compassion beyond your close circle. Simple actions like making eye contact and smiling at strangers can bridge divides, foster community spirit, and remind you of our shared humanity.

CHAPTER RECAP

In this chapter, we covered the basics of empathy and the different types, as well as contrasting empathy to sympathy. Developing empathy and improving social skills are essential for fostering strong relationships and effective communication with others. By honing your empathy skills, you can better understand and share the feelings of those around you. Likewise, enhancing your social skills enables you to interact seamlessly and harmoniously in various social settings. Here are a few strategies to try that can help improve your social skills:

ACTION ITEMS

Effective conversation techniques: Having effective conversation skills is a cornerstone of strong social skills. Intentionally do the following 3 times or more this week:

- Summarize in your notebook/journal the who/what/when/where/why of your conversation that involved intentional active listening.
- Practice active listening, which involves giving your full attention to the person speaking and genuinely engaging with what they are saying.
- After you have listened to them, summarize and paraphrase their words back to them to demonstrate that you are actively processing and understanding their message.
- Strive for a balance between speaking and listening so that the conversation is mutually beneficial and engaging.

Asking open-ended questions: During the 3 conversational situations above, ask questions that go beyond simple "yes" or "no" answers. These types of questions encourage the other person to provide more detailed and thoughtful responses, allowing for a more comprehensive understanding of their thoughts and feelings. Open-ended questions can foster connection and create opportunities for exploration and discovery within the conversation.

Body language and facial expressions: During the 3 conversational situations above:

- Note and demonstrate how nonverbal communication plays a crucial role in social interactions.
- Be mindful of your body language and facial expressions, as they can convey both empathy and interest or withdrawal and disengagement.
- Maintain an open posture, leaning slightly towards the person you are conversing with, as it signals attentiveness and openness.
- Make eye contact to demonstrate that you are fully present and engaged in the conversation.
- Use facial expressions that reflect your emotions and show empathy towards the other person's experiences.

Practicing these strategies can help you improve your social skills and create a positive and empathetic presence in your interactions with others. The next chapter will discuss how you can master your social skills through effective strategies.

CHAPTER 5
RELATIONSHIP MANAGEMENT: MASTERING AND APPLYING SOCIAL SKILLS

Relationship Management is the culmination of getting a grip on your emotional intelligence. Self-awareness leads to self-management, and social awareness combined with self-management allows you to effectively manage relationships. You rely on your relationships to maintain your sense of worth, security, love, and belonging. Your mental health and even physical health mirror the health of your relationships. You must possess the social skills necessary to build and nurture all your relationships, be they intimate, familial, paternal, personal, or professional.

Social skills are dynamic; you can develop and improve your social skills and relationship management at any stage of life. Various strategies and techniques can improve your social competencies and make you more effective in your interactions with others.

One effective method is peer mentoring, where individuals learn from and support one another in a mutually beneficial relationship. You and your peer mentor can provide guidance, feedback, and encouragement, helping each other develop your social skills in a safe and supportive environment.

Another approach is social skills training, which involves structured activities and exercises designed to enhance specific social skills. These trainings may cover a wide range of skills, including active listening, assertiveness, empathy, conflict resolution, and nonverbal communication. By systematically practicing these skills, you will become more proficient in navigating social situations and building positive relationships.

Therapy can also be a valuable resource for individuals looking to improve their social skills. Your therapist can provide a safe space for exploring and addressing any underlying issues that may be affecting your social interactions. Your therapist can also offer guidance and strategies for developing your communication skills and managing social anxiety or other related challenges you may be facing.

However, the key to mastering social skills and relationship management lies in real-world application. Interacting with others offers you the most solid potential for growth. Engaging in dialogues, joining group activities, and working with others on projects are all invaluable experiences that help you hone social skills. By proactively seeking and embracing these situations, you will develop stronger relationships and enrich your life and their lives with deeper connections.

Acknowledging the importance of social skills and actively working on them can lead to more satisfying relationships, both personal and professional. By committing to ongoing development, you can better navigate the intricacies of human interactions with enhanced understanding, trust, and cooperation.

THE ART OF COMMUNICATION

Communication is often referred to as an art, and rightfully so. Just like a painter starting with a blank canvas, we begin with the objective of conveying our message to others. We have the freedom to paint any picture we desire in order to communicate effectively. Many people believe that they only have a limited set of brushes to work with when painting their communication picture. However, experienced communicators understand that there are numerous tools at their disposal, and they are adept at utilizing each one to their advantage.

Communication, like painting, can be enhanced by utilizing a variety of tools. The key is to be aware of these tools and to use them purposefully. The more skilled you become at leveraging these tools, the more effective your communication skills will become. You looked at communication earlier with its bearing on empathy; now, we will take a more focused look at this keystone that supports strong relationships.

The tools of communication can be broadly categorized into two main categories: verbal and nonverbal. Each category encompasses several techniques that can greatly enhance your ability to communicate effectively. Effective use of both powers your overall communication skills.

In the verbal category, employing techniques such as active listening, effective questioning, and using appropriate language can significantly enhance your verbal communication. Active listening involves giving your full attention to the speaker, displaying interest, and providing thoughtful responses. Skillful questioning helps to facilitate deeper conversations and allows for a better understanding of the other person's perspective. Once you know where they are coming from, appropriate language, tone, and clarity in your speech can ensure that your message is conveyed accurately and with impact.

Nonverbal communication plays a crucial role as well. Body language, facial expressions, and gestures can either reinforce or contradict your verbal communication. Maintaining an open posture, making eye contact, and using appropriate facial expressions can convey trust, sincerity, and engagement. Conversely, closed-off body language or inconsistent nonverbal cues can create barriers to effective communication.

EFFECTIVE COMMUNICATION

Effective communication is a two-way process that requires the active participation of both the sender and the receiver. It is not simply about conveying information but about creating a mutual understanding between the parties involved. Communication involves the sender sharing their thoughts and ideas, which are influenced by their perspectives, attitudes, and assumptions. On the other side, the receiver interprets the message based on their own unique experiences and values.

To achieve true communication, there must be a continuous flow of understanding between both the sender and the receiver, forming a feedback loop. Skilled communicators understand the importance of considering the information they share and the timing of their delivery. They value honesty and transparency, and they actively seek to clarify misunderstandings as they arise. They are also sensitive to the emotions of the people they are communicating with and try to address them empathetically.

A key skill of effective communicators is the ability to listen with both their intellect and their heart. Instead of simply hearing the words being spoken, they actively strive to understand the underlying message and emotions behind them. They approach listening without judgment or defensiveness, creating a safe space for the other person to express themselves fully. By actively listening and seeking to comprehend, they can respond in a way that is meaningful and beneficial to everyone involved.

Skilled communicators carefully choose their words to ensure that they provide others with the necessary information. They understand that clear, honest, and focused exchanges of ideas and information lead to the most favorable outcomes. They are mindful of the impact their words may have on others and take responsibility for their communication, striving to be clear, concise, and respectful in their delivery.

Barriers to Effective Communication

Barriers to effective communication can hinder the exchange of information between the sender and receiver, leading to confusion and miscommunication. Let's take a detailed look at some of the common barriers to effective communication.

Semantic barriers are obstacles to communication through the words used that distort the intended meaning of a message. Misunderstandings can emerge from various circumstances that create a semantic gap between the sender and the receiver. Such circumstances include, but are not limited to, differences in language, educational backgrounds, or cultural norms. "It's a matter of semantics..." is a phrase you may have heard before when the sender senses the receiver has misinterpreted the message.

Technical language can also act as a language barrier. If the sender uses technical terms or jargon that the receiver is not familiar with, it can create confusion and misunderstanding, impairing effective communication. "Just say it in plain English…" is a phrase the receiver might use to convey a problem with the message from the sender.

Psychological barriers play a significant role in interpersonal communication. The mental state of both the sender and receiver can impact their understanding of the information being conveyed, often leading to misunderstandings. People in distress have trouble absorbing what is said. Short, simple directions often help when trying to calm someone or communicate with them.

Inadequate attention from the receiver can also contribute to communication barriers. If the receiver is not attentive during the communication process, they may not fully grasp the information being conveyed, leading to a breakdown in effective communication. Premature evaluation of information by the receiver, sometimes before it is fully transmitted, can create barriers to communication. The receiver may form premature conclusions, which can distort the original message. Additionally, when information is passed through multiple sources, the final message can become distorted as each receiver may not retain all the information that was conveyed, creating further communication barriers.

Organizational barriers arise from the structure, rules, and regulations within an organization. The relationship between superiors and subordinates can hinder the free flow of communication. Complex organizational structures and multiple managers can make it difficult to convey information accurately, leading to miscommunication.

Cultural barriers stem from differences in cultures worldwide. Certain terms or actions that are considered harmless in one culture may be perceived as offensive or inappropriate in another. Divergent beliefs and values can also create barriers to effective communication.

Various factors can cause physical barriers, such as faulty equipment, noise, closed doors, or cabins. These physical elements can distort the information being sent from the sender to the receiver, leading to improper communication.

Physiological barriers occur when a sender or receiver is unable to express or receive messages clearly due to physiological issues. Conditions like dyslexia or nerve disorders can interfere with speech or hearing, creating barriers to effective communication.

Real-Life Examples of Effective Communication

Bridgewater Associates, one of the leading investment management firms globally, has implemented a unique approach to maintaining good internal communication—recording every meeting. This company policy serves several functions, including being a means of communication, a tool for learning and development, and a way to promote precision and reduce politicking.

Recording every meeting enables Bridgewater Associates to explore mistakes quickly and efficiently. By using communication as a tool for investigating errors, the company can accurately identify the root cause of any issue. This approach creates an environment that encourages problem-solving and allows the company to develop effective solutions.

Every employee has access to the recorded meetings, which promotes transparency and ensures that everyone is on the same page. This approach also provides a valuable learning tool for employees, allowing them to develop a deeper understanding of the company's operations and strategies.

Moreover, recording every meeting can serve as evidence in case of any disputes or misunderstandings. This approach promotes accountability and strengthens the company's governance framework.

Strategies for Improving Communication Skills

Effective communication is a valuable skill that involves delivering information concisely, maintaining the interest of your audience, and ensuring that all necessary information is conveyed. Here are some strategies to enhance your communication effectiveness:

- **Tailor your message to your audience:** Understanding your audience's interests and needs is essential. By addressing their specific concerns and speaking directly about what matters to them, you can engage their curiosity and motivate their desire to understand and interact with the information. Consider the perspectives and knowledge levels of your audience to communicate in a way that resonates with them.
- **Keep it simple:** Avoid using unnecessary words or jargon that may confuse or bore your audience. Remember that they are hearing the information for the first time while you already know it. Keeping your message concise and straightforward makes it easier for others to understand and retain the information. Focus on delivering key points and avoid unnecessary elaboration.
- **Utilize face-to-face communication:** Whenever possible, opt for face-to-face communication. In-person interactions provide multiple layers of information, such as nonverbal cues, tone of voice, and facial expressions. These additional dimensions contribute to a richer communication experience and help foster better

understanding. Face-to-face communication also allows for immediate feedback and clarification, reducing the chance of miscommunication.
- **Maintain eye contact:** When speaking to someone directly, eye contact plays a critical role in gauging the effectiveness of your communication. It provides valuable feedback on whether your message is being understood if the person is distracted, worried, or confused. By maintaining eye contact, you can adjust your communication approach in real time to address any potential barriers or misunderstandings.

NONVERBAL COMMUNICATION

Nonverbal communication encompasses the use of various nonverbal cues such as gestures, tone of voice, facial expressions, body posture, and more. While verbal communication is explicit and direct, nonverbal cues often carry implicit messages that can reveal underlying emotions, attitudes, and intentions. Understanding and interpreting nonverbal cues is crucial because they provide valuable insights that complement and sometimes even contradict verbal communication. Here's why nonverbal communication cues are essential to identify and understand:

- **Emotional expression:** Nonverbal cues often convey emotions more effectively than words alone. Facial expressions, such as a smile or a frown, can instantly reveal joy, anger, sadness, or surprise, enhancing our understanding of the speaker's feelings.
- **Tone of voice:** The way words are spoken can convey meaning beyond the actual words. The tone of voice, including volume, pitch, and intonation, can indicate sarcasm, enthusiasm, boredom, or aggression.

Understanding these cues helps us interpret the true intent and attitude behind the verbal message.

- **Body language:** Posture, gestures, and body movements can provide insights into a person's confidence, interest, engagement, or discomfort. For example, crossed arms may indicate defensiveness or detachment, while open and relaxed body language suggests receptiveness and attentiveness.
- **Cultural nuances:** Nonverbal cues can vary across different cultures. For instance, a thumbs-up gesture may be seen as positive in one culture but offensive in another. Being aware of cultural differences in nonverbal communication helps prevent misunderstandings and fosters effective cross-cultural interactions.
- **Detecting deception:** Nonverbal cues often reveal when someone is being dishonest or hiding something. Micro-expressions, subtle changes in facial expressions that occur in a fraction of a second, can signify concealed emotions that contrast with the spoken message. Recognizing these cues aids in identifying deception and understanding the speaker's true intentions.
- **Enhancing communication:** Nonverbal communication complements verbal messages and provides additional context, making communication more nuanced and expressive. It helps convey sincerity, empathy, and trust, creating stronger individual connections and fostering effective interpersonal relationships.

The Importance of Body Language

Body language is critical in effective communication as it enables individuals to express their emotions and feelings nonverbally. How you act and sound significantly impacts how others perceive you, and nonverbal cues can put them at ease, draw them towards you, establish trust, or even create a negative impression.

Body language is an essential part of communication that is not limited to personal interactions with family, spouses, or children. It is equally vital in professional settings, and individuals who are aware of its significance can benefit. Understanding nonverbal communication can:

- Help you communicate your ideas, opinions, and emotions more effectively by using gestures, expressions, and tone of voice that convey the intended message better than words alone.
- Enable you to better connect with others by demonstrating attentiveness and engagement through active listening, maintaining eye contact, and open body language. This process helps build rapport and foster stronger relationships.
- Facilitate stronger bonds with colleagues, clients, and stakeholders by enhancing the quality of interactions and fostering a more favorable impression. Increase trust and clarity by aligning your verbal and nonverbal communication, which helps avoid misunderstandings and conflicts.

The Role of Nonverbal Communication in Building Relationships

Nonverbal communication is a crucial factor in building and maintaining relationships with others. When used effectively, nonverbal cues help us understand each other's thoughts and emotions and increase the level of respect between individuals. Appropriately conveyed nonverbal cues also establish trust within a relationship.

It is important to remain mindful of nonverbal communication when interacting with others, as it can significantly impact whether a relationship succeeds or fails. Heightened nonverbal awareness is essential, especially when engaging in conversation with another person. The more sensitivity one develops towards nonverbal cues, the more effective they can be in communication, which, in turn, allows them to create stronger relationships with others.

How you position yourself when sitting or standing at work can say a lot about your attitude and level of attention in different situations. Sitting or standing up straight demonstrates that you are actively engaged in a conversation and gives off an impression of confidence, especially in an interview setting.

For example, imagine that you have been assigned the responsibility of presenting a new idea to your supervisor, and you want to communicate your message effectively. In this situation, you can choose to sit or stand with your shoulders pulled back, which will not only convey confidence but also emphasize why you strongly believe that your idea will greatly benefit the company. By maintaining good posture and displaying a strong presence, you can leave a lasting impression and increase the chances of your idea being well-received.

CONFLICT RESOLUTION

Conflict resolution refers to the process of finding a peaceful and satisfactory resolution to a disagreement or conflict between two or more parties. Such conflicts can arise from personal differences, financial disputes, political disagreements, or emotional tensions.

In these situations, negotiation often emerges as the most effective approach to resolving the dispute. Negotiation is a form of communication and discussion where the parties involved collaborate to reach a mutually agreed solution.

There are three primary goals of negotiation in conflict resolution:

1. **Finding a solution that all parties involved can agree to.** This statement means that the outcome should be acceptable to everyone, ensuring a fair and balanced resolution.
2. **Working as efficiently as possible to find this solution.** Time is often of the essence, as prolonged conflicts can be detrimental to relationships, productivity, and overall well-being.
3. **Improving the relationship between the conflicting parties.** The aim is to foster understanding, empathy, and cooperation rather than exacerbating negative emotions or creating further divisions.

Engaging in conflict resolution through negotiation has several benefits for all parties involved. By participating in negotiation, each side can gain more than they would by simply walking away or refusing to engage in the process. Additionally, negotiation can provide a platform to access resources or benefits that may have otherwise been unattainable.

Strategies for Effective Conflict Resolution

Understanding the underlying interests in a conflict is crucial for effective conflict resolution. Often, groups tend to waste time and energy by solely focusing on positional bargaining, where they argue and defend their rigid positions rather than explain their interests. This approach limits the possibilities for negotiation and makes it difficult for parties to let go of their positions without feeling embarrassed or losing face. It becomes more about saving face than finding a suitable resolution.

A more productive approach is to explore and identify the interests of all parties involved. By understanding the underlying motivations and concerns, it becomes easier to communicate and find mutually acceptable solutions. It is valuable to look beyond the stated positions and delve into the reasons behind those positions. This understanding opens up more opportunities for creative problem-solving.

Once you have a clear understanding of the interests of both parties and have established effective communication channels with the opposition, you can begin to consider potential solutions. Examining the list of interests for both sides, it is common to identify shared or overlapping interests. For example, both groups may desire stability and public respect. Identifying common interests provides a solid foundation for working toward a resolution that addresses the needs of all parties involved.

To facilitate productive discussions and brainstorming sessions, it is important to plan the meeting carefully. Start by clearly stating the purpose of the meeting, ensuring everyone understands its focus and objectives. Opt for a smaller group of around five to eight individuals to encourage active participation and allow for meaningful dialogue. It is beneficial to hold the meeting in a different environment than the usual setting to promote a fresh perspective. Choosing a comfortable and safe setting, preferably informal, will encourage open communication and cooperation.

In addition, it is crucial to find an unbiased facilitator who can ensure the meeting's structure and flow without expressing personal opinions regarding the conflict. This facilitator can guide the discussions, helping the parties explore their interests further, generate ideas, and navigate toward a resolution fairly and impartially.

CHAPTER RECAP

Relationship Management, Pillar 4, is the culmination of getting a grip on your emotional intelligence. Self-awareness leads to self-management, and social awareness combined with self-management allows you to manage relationships. Communication is key to expressing yourself, understanding others, and developing relationships. This chapter looked at various social skills, the art and development of effective communication, the importance of nonverbal communication, and goals and strategies for conflict resolution. Here are some exercises you can do to enhance your nonverbal communication and interpersonal skills.

ACTION ITEMS

Interactive games are a fun way to build your social skills and relationship management. The following are some activities you can try with a few of your friends:

Charades is an enjoyable game that involves acting out words or phrases without speaking. One player selects a word or phrase and acts it out using gestures, facial expressions, and body movements while the other players try to guess what it is. The game encourages nonverbal communication and helps improve your ability to convey meaning through actions.

Several commercial games provide for good relationship challenges and development. Trivial Pursuit, Quickwits, Cards Against Humanity, and Apples to Apples are a few that might work well, depending on the social setting.

Friendly card games do well to develop your skills as well. Avoid serious betting games and be sure everyone understands the rules of the game.

Organize a small group of your friends, pick a game together and give it a try. Have fun, test your sporting attitude, and note the verbal and non-verbal communication that goes on as you play.

* * *

Don't forget… BONUS exercises to help you Get A Grip On Your Emotional Intelligence are available to you FREE.

Send me an email at:

KennyLeeBooks@gmail.com

and I will send you a bonus set of exercises along with updates for your Emotional Intelligence journey into your future.

If you have a specific area of EI you would like to work on, let me know via email and I will send you some exercises specific to your area of concern.

To your continued progress!

Your Life. Your Health. Your Journey… Take Action!

~ *Kenny Lee*

* * *

CHAPTER 6
MOTIVATION AND EMOTIONAL INTELLIGENCE

"All our dreams can come true if we have the courage to pursue them."

WALT DISNEY

Self-motivation is the most powerful type of motivation. Being self-motivated extends beyond the capability of completing tasks listed on your agenda. It involves a profound comprehension of your personal motivational factors and what fails to inspire you. This form of motivation originates from within, instead of depending on external influences or guidance from others. Your motivation is powered by your own interests, principles, and passions, not by conforming to the expectations or agendas of others.

The essence of self-motivation lies in self-awareness, recognizing your motivational triggers and sources of inspiration. It's about identifying what ignites your enthusiasm and commitment and then shaping your objectives and actions to align with these insights. When self-motivated, you harness your inner enthusiasm and show initiative without the need for external approval or incentives.

You fuel your fire from within to self-manage your life toward the goals you desire. Your direction, your goals. Not someone else's idea or plan for where you should go or who you should be.

Embrace the power of self-motivation to steer your own course and own up to your achievements. You will set significant goals that resonate with your deepest ambitions and values. Through self-motivation, you become the primary force behind your successes, independent of reliance on external sources for motivation or direction.

THE DRIVE WITHIN

Self-motivation is the innate drive that pushes you towards accomplishing specific objectives. It acts as an internal catalyst, maintaining your motivation and dedication, even amidst difficulties and hurdles. For example, if someone aims to run for 20 minutes, their self-motivation encourages them to overcome tiredness and fulfill this goal. This concept encompasses discipline, resolve, and concentration in realizing personal ambitions and dreams.

Inherently, self-motivation stems from your own mindset, values, beliefs, and aspirations. It is independent of external elements like the opinions of others, rewards, or potential consequences. Self-motivation empowers you to take control of your life, work towards your personal aims, and seize emerging opportunities. This process demands consistent effort, commitment, and a persistent zeal for success.

To sustain self-motivation, you need self-discipline, which involves adhering to your plans despite encountering challenges. Self-discipline helps you stay on track with your goals and avoid distractions that could impede progress. Equally important is genuine self-confidence, crucial for self-motivation, as it fosters belief in your own abilities and potential to realize set goals. Ultimately, self-motivation is a key element in effectively achieving personal and professional objectives.

INTRINSIC VS. EXTRINSIC MOTIVATION

Intrinsic motivation stems from your internal desire and pleasure gained from participating in an activity. It involves engaging in actions for the sheer joy and personal gratification they provide, rather than for external rewards or due to outside pressures like deadlines or incentives. The essence of intrinsic motivation lies in you deriving value and meaning from the activity itself, making the act its own reward.

This type of motivation is intimately connected with your personal development and a sense of commitment. It is fueled by a profound belief in the significance and relevance of the task or activity at hand. For instance, playing sports for the inherent enjoyment and satisfaction it offers, working overtime out of a strong personal conviction in the task's value, using positive affirmations for self-improvement, or investing money to achieve financial freedom exemplify intrinsic motivation.

Conversely, extrinsic motivation revolves around external rewards or avoiding penalties. It pertains to actions taken by you with the primary intention of gaining something valuable in return or evading negative outcomes. This kind of motivation is typically motivated by monetary rewards, status, recognition, or the aspiration to fulfill external expectations.

Examples of extrinsic motivation are studying to get good grades, assisting others with the hope of receiving commendation or recognition, volunteering to enhance one's resume or public persona, or shopping at a specific store to benefit from loyalty program rewards.

The Role of Motivation in Achieving Goals

Motivation plays a vital role in your life, driving you to alter your behavior, acquire new skills, think innovatively, set and accomplish objectives, develop interests, plan effectively, refine your abilities, and deepen your involvement in various life aspects. By harnessing the insights of motivational science, you can effectively inspire employees at work, coach athletes to excel, guide children towards independence and ambition, support clients in their personal development, and stimulate students' interest in their studies.

In the absence of motivation, you risk becoming stagnant, lacking the impetus to seize new prospects or implement necessary life changes. Motivation acts as the internal force that moves you forward, fosters personal growth, and helps you confront challenges with a constructive attitude. It is through motivation that you unlock your greatest potential, achieve success in your pursuits, and lead a full, enriched life.

Your goals, both personal and professional, depend on motivation to achieve worthwhile success. Whether facing opportunities or challenges, motivation is key in helping you manage difficulties and optimize your capabilities. Motivation is the critical tool that equips you to push through obstacles and adapt to changes and new situations to get what you desire for yourself and others.

CULTIVATING SELF-MOTIVATION

Cultivating self-motivation can be a complex task as it necessitates discovering your internal drive… discovering the WHY for what you want from life, your Deep Purpose. Why do I want this? Why is it important? You may be tempted to ascribe your stalled progress or lack of achievement to external factors or to hold others responsible. Take a step back and re-examine your WHY, your Deep Purpose.

Also, genuine self-motivation entails accepting responsibility for your decisions and actions. Although external circumstances and support from friends can offer momentary motivation, the onus is on you to exert the effort required and actively work towards your objectives. You have the capability to take control of your life and confront any issues that might be obstructing your advancement.

There are times when, despite having a clear vision and purpose, despite re-examining your Deep Purpose, you still experience a lack of motivation. In such situations, it might be beneficial to reevaluate your direction and consider embarking on a new path. If your current motivations aren't sufficiently stimulating, it could be an opportunity to redefine your goals and foster a renewed sense of purpose. Progress is crucial, and any steps taken towards self-improvement signify advancement over inaction.

Your own self-imposed limitations often represent the most significant barriers in your life. A lack of self-motivation frequently arises from the belief that you are not inherently capable. It's crucial, therefore, to transform these negative perceptions into positive affirmations. You can train your mind to adopt empowering beliefs about your abilities. Recognizing and altering negative self-talk into motivating and empowering thoughts is vital for your personal growth and motivation.

Limitations and Belief

As a man observed a camp of elephants, he was struck by the peculiar sight before him. These massive creatures, known for their strength and power, were not confined within cages or chains. Instead, they were tied with a thin rope to a simple pole in the ground. Perplexed by this seemingly flimsy restraint, the man approached the trainer to inquire about the elephants' lack of escape attempts.

The trainer enlightened the man with a fascinating explanation. He revealed that this method of restraint had been employed since the elephants were mere babies. At that young age, the relatively weak rope was sufficient to prevent them from wandering away. Over time, as the elephants grew into majestic adults, they continued to be bound by the same flimsy rope that had confined them in their infancy.

When the man pressed further, asking why the elephants didn't utilize their immense strength to break free, the trainer imparted a profound revelation. He explained that the elephants, conditioned from a young age, had come to believe that they were incapable of breaking the rope. This deeply ingrained belief prevented them from even attempting to escape, resigning them to stay within the confines of the camp despite their physical prowess and intelligence.

The story of these elephants serves as a poignant metaphor for the limitations that we often place on ourselves. Just like the mighty elephants, we can become trapped by our own beliefs and perceptions, accepting constraints that are merely illusions. The elephants' mental confinement was a result of their early experiences and the false notion that they were powerless against the rope. Similarly, in our own lives, our self-imposed limitations can prevent us from realizing our full potential and hinder us from exploring new opportunities.

Reflect on your own beliefs and question the boundaries you have set for yourself. Challenge your self-imposed limitations that prevent you from attempting new endeavors or embracing personal growth. By recognizing and confronting these limiting beliefs, you can break free from the metaphorical ropes that bind you and unlock your true potential.

SETTING AND ACHIEVING GOALS

Establishing goals is essential for achieving success. Without well-defined goals, you may find yourself without a clear focus or direction, resulting in a sense of aimlessness. Goal setting empowers you to steer your life's course and offers tangible benchmarks to assess your progress towards our desired outcomes.

It is crucial to reflect on your WHY, your Deep Purpose, and the significance of your goals. Goals should hold meaning and resonate with your personal values and dreams. For instance, if accumulating wealth is your goal, a million dollars in the bank might symbolize success. However, if your ultimate aim is to contribute to charitable causes, then the significance of the wealth shifts. Your goals should not only be significant but also serve as a source of inspiration and motivation, propelling you toward action and accomplishment.

For goals to be effective, they need to be explicit, detailed, and specific. Broad or ambiguous goals lack the clarity needed to provide direction or formulate a path to success. Goals should act as navigational tools, offering a distinct destination. Precisely defining what we want to achieve enables us to visualize the end result and identify the steps needed to reach it.

Incorporating quantifiable elements into our goals is crucial for monitoring progress and assessing our success. Without measurable criteria, gauging whether we are making substantial progress towards our goals becomes challenging. For example, a goal like "reduce expenses" is too vague to effectively track. In contrast, setting a goal to decrease expenses by a specific percentage within a defined period gives us a tangible metric to measure our progress and acknowledge our achievements.

Measuring our successes provides a sense of accomplishment and continued motivation. It offers recognition for our efforts and serves as a testament to what we can achieve. Celebrating achievements, whether they are modest gains made in a short period or significant milestones reached over years, is essential. Having measurable goals not only allows us to rejoice in our successes but also strengthens our belief in our ability to achieve our aspirations.

Be SMART About It

Defining your goals through the "SMART" acronym has become a standard in corporate training and personal improvement. SMART goals give you definition, direction, and timing.

a) Specific

Your goals should be as specific as possible. "I want to get fit" is less effective than "I want to lose 10 pounds in 3 months."

b) Measurable

What doesn't get measured doesn't get managed. Find a way to track your progress. For example, instead of saying, "I want to read more," say, "I want to read one book a month."

c) Achievable

Your goals should stretch you, but not break you. Be realistic about what you can achieve within a given time frame.

d) Relevant

The goals you set should be relevant to the direction you want your life or career to take. Relevance gives you the motivation to achieve your goal.

e) Time-bound

Every goal needs a timeframe. Having a deadline creates a sense of urgency and can act as a powerful motivator.

Consider John, a mid-level executive aiming for a leadership role in his company. John sets a SMART goal: "I will improve my leadership skills by completing a 12-week management training course within the next six months." This goal is specific, measurable, achievable, relevant, and time-bound, helping John map out a clear path toward career advancement.

Your Goals are Yours

Your goals are an extension of your individuality. They should resonate with your values and aspirations, your WHY, not someone else's. This is VERY important. You be you.

It's easy to compare your journey to those around you but remember that every individual's path is unique. Base your goals on your personal criteria, not someone else's achievements.

Being authentic in setting your goals ensures that achieving them will bring you fulfillment. Goals rooted in authenticity are more sustainable in the long run.

Societal pressures can often steer you away from your authentic self. Be wary of setting goals simply because you feel it's what you 'should' be doing according to societal norms.

Take Emily, who grew up in a family of doctors. The societal and familial expectation was that she would also enter the medical field. However, her passion was in environmental science. She asserted herself, telling her family of her WHY, her aspirations, her goals. By setting her own authentic direction and goals, Emily was able to break away from societal and familial expectations to find true fulfillment in her work as a bioengineer creating innovative technology to clean up petroleum hazards and waste.

CHAPTER RECAP

Pure motivation must come from within. Through self-awareness of your essential WHY, your Deep Purpose, along with your self-management of setting and owning your goals and and achieving them, you will power your motivation and get where you want to go in life.

In this chapter, Motivation and Emotional Intelligence, you looked at the drive within yourself, intrinsic versus extrinsic motivation, cultivating your self-motivation, and setting and achieving goals. SMART goals. Your goals.

The action items below are the on-ramp for the road to success. It is up to you to put the vehicle in gear and drive.

ACTION ITEMS

Using your notebook/journal, review your WHY and Deep Purpose, then set your Deep Goals using these exercises:

1. Define your WHY/Deep Purpose. Start with a blank page, and for 10 minutes brainstorming ideas, fill the page with ideas of your WHY, your Deep Purpose, for where you want to go in life.

- Review this list and circle the top 3 WHY items that best fit your vision.
- On another blank page, list one of these top 3 WHY/Deep Purpose items and distill it further. An example:

  - Deep Purpose – Live a minimalist life
    - Why? - because I want to rid my life of clutter and unused things
    - Why? - because I want to simplify my life and be less materialistic
    - Why? - so I can spend time, effort, and money on what is important to me and my family
    - Why? - to build better relationships with my partner, family, and friends
    - Why? - because these relationships are most important to me in life
    - Why? - because life is meaningless without them

- Do this for the other two of your top 3 items

Save your lists for future reference. Review every 6 months or so to gauge how far you have come or where your priorities and vision may have changed.

2. Define your Deep Goals. You need Deep Goals, directions for your personal journey on the highway to your Deep Purpose. The 6 Standards of Deep Goals and their considerations to balance your life and support your Deep Purpose are as follows:

- Health – physical and mental health, your holistic wellness
- Wealth – debt, savings, investments, college plans, retirement plans
- Work – your job, your side hustle, your entrepreneurial dreams
- Family – immediate family, extended family
- Personal – for yourself, selfish because they are for you
- Relationship – spouse, partner, significant other

On a blank page, pick one area, let's say "Health," and brainstorm ideas for Deep Goals in this area for 10 minutes. Just ideas, not specifics. That comes next.

From these ideas, pick your top three to consider. Of these top three, pick the one Deep Goal that is the priority for you right now. Develop that one raw goal into a SMART goal, being Specific, Measurable, Achievable, Relevant, and Time-bound.

Repeat this Deep Goal definition for the other 5 Standards.

Save your brainstorming ideas for later reference. Once you attain one of your Deep Goals, you can use the list for that particular Standard to select and develop the next Deep Goal you will achieve.

When this exercise is complete, you will have Deep Goals for all 6 Standards. Take the list and put it in a prominent place where you will see it often. Frame it and dress it up if you like. Make it yours.

When journaling, strive to review these Deep Goals at least weekly. Stick to your timeframe for completion. Review your Deep Purpose and these Deep Goals whenever you feel your motivation waning.

A habit tracker is another excellent exercise to help you stay motivated. Keeping a log of your habits and goals and tracking your progress can significantly increase your chances of success. Fortunately, there are many creative ways to set up a habit tracker, including using checkmarks on your calendar or creating doodles to represent your goals. The key is to make it a daily practice and track your progress consistently.

Create a vision board. This activity is an opportunity to get creative and literally visualize your Deep Goals. You can cut out pictures from magazines or use different fonts to create your vision board. Once completed, hang it somewhere prominent where you can see it daily to remind yourself of your aspirations.

Now that you have a foundation on self-motivation, let's look at motivating others, a key point in relationship management. As a motivator of others, you are a leader. This may have a formal designation such as a job title or be informal as a member of a group or team that people look to for leadership. The next chapter is all about leadership and emotional intelligence — Why developed EI results in being a successful leader.

CHAPTER 7
LEADERSHIP AND EMOTIONAL INTELLIGENCE

In today's workplace, EI is highly prized as an interpersonal skill. Since the recession of 2008, smaller staff, higher stress, and uncertainties of the future have led employers to place greater emphasis on EI in prospective employees. Studies found that over 70% of employers view EI as more critical than IQ or technical skills when evaluating job applicants (Hunt, 2011). Up until 2020, global emotional intelligence was on the rise. But then the pandemic took over our collective psyche, and a decline has persisted since. This chapter will delve into how leaders improve their EI and how this enhancement can boost you to excel in your role, even as the rest of the world struggles to recover.

Key elements of your EI in leadership mirror those elements of your personal EI: Self-awareness, self-management, social awareness, and relationship management. The technical abilities that contributed to your initial career advancement may not be sufficient for future leadership positions. To be an effective leader, it's crucial for you to focus on emotional intelligence. Your EI significantly influences your ability to mentor teams, handle stress, provide constructive feedback, and collaborate effectively with others.

Leaders with high levels of emotional intelligence are adept at fostering a positive work atmosphere, motivating team members to reach their objectives, effectively resolving conflicts, and adjusting to changing environments. Conversely, leaders with lower EI often encounter difficulties in interpersonal relationships, leading to subpar team performance, increased staff turnover, and diminished job satisfaction.

EMOTIONAL INTELLIGENCE IN LEADERSHIP

When envisioning an ideal leader, certain traits often come to mind. You might picture a leader who remains calm and composed in tough situations. Or perhaps you think of someone who has gained their team's complete trust, listens attentively, is easily approachable, and consistently makes informed decisions. These attributes are typically found in individuals with high emotional intelligence. Well-developed EI allows you to comprehend and manage not only your own emotions but also those of others.

The base component of EI is self-awareness, being attuned to your emotions and understanding how your behavior and feelings can affect the people around you. As a leader, self-awareness also means you have a clear grasp of your strengths and limitations, and you demonstrate humility in your conduct and interactions.

Leaders who excel in self-management are skilled at keeping their emotions and impulses in check. They are less likely to lash out verbally, make hasty or emotion-driven decisions, stereotype people, or compromise their principles. Your self-management entails managing your emotions, behaviors, and decisions effectively, even in stressful or high-pressure scenarios.

By developing self-awareness and self-management, you can gain a deeper insight into yourself as a leader and your influence on others, both those you lead and also those you follow. This level of comprehension leads to social awareness, allowing you to respond appropriately to diverse situations, forge strong relationships, make judicious decisions, and foster a positive and inclusive workplace atmosphere. Relationship management as a leader involves seeking feedback, assessing the current situation, using EI to adapt to changing situations, and continual engagement with your professional relationships.

LEADERSHIP STYLES AND EI

The work environment and culture have a significant impact on employee performance. The most effective work climates that drive performance typically exhibit six key characteristics:

- **Clear Expectations** – Employees should have a clear understanding of what their managers expect from them and how their work contributes to the overall goals of the organization. Clear expectations help employees align their efforts and focus on achieving their objectives.
- **Valid Goals** – Challenging but attainable goals are crucial for fostering employee motivation and performance. Goals that push employees to stretch their abilities while still being within their reach can drive them to perform at their best.
- **Innovation and Creativity** – A company should embrace new ideas and encourage innovation and creativity among its employees. This openness to new ideas breeds a culture of learning and experimentation, allowing employees to contribute their unique perspectives and making the organization more adaptable to change.

- **Empowerment and Accountability** – When employees are enabled to take ownership of their work and are held accountable for their actions and outcomes, they feel a sense of responsibility and are motivated to deliver high-quality results.
- **Recognition and Reward** — Effective leaders acknowledge and appreciate their team members' efforts and achievements. They also provide guidance and support to help employees continuously improve their performance.
- **Belonging** – A strong sense of pride and camaraderie among team members is essential. When people feel a sense of belonging and work together toward a common purpose, they are more likely to be motivated, collaborate effectively, and strive for shared success.

Leaders play a vital role in creating and maintaining this positive work climate. The most effective leaders utilize a range of leadership styles to achieve these characteristics:

- Visionary leaders provide long-term direction and context.
- Participative leaders build commitment and generate new ideas through collaboration.
- Coaching leaders support the long-term development of their employees.
- Affiliative leaders create trust and harmony within the team.
- Pacesetting leaders set high standards to accomplish tasks.
- Directive leaders focus on gaining immediate compliance.

Importance of Adaptability in Leadership

Transforming into a flexible leader is a continuous journey that demands ongoing effort and practice. It entails honing the skill to respond adeptly to a range of situations, both major and minor. Adaptable leaders are characterized by specific qualities that enable them to manage change effectively.

A key characteristic of such leaders is their readiness to exert additional effort in unfamiliar and unpredictable scenarios. They welcome these changes and capitalize on the opportunities they present, even if it requires exceeding their typical duties.

Another significant quality of adaptable leaders is maintaining a positive attitude, even in challenging circumstances. They tackle obstacles with a proactive mindset and inspire their team to adopt a similar approach, regardless of the situation's apparent difficulties.

These leaders are also known for their flexibility in various aspects, such as scheduling, communication styles, and methods. They are open to altering their plans, objectives, and strategies to align with their team's needs and the organization's objectives. Their adaptability in communication ensures they effectively convey their message to different audiences.

A willingness to embrace and apply new, advantageous technologies marks another important trait of adaptable leaders. They actively seek innovative tools and methods that can enhance their work quality and increase their team's efficiency.

Lastly, adaptable leaders are proficient in re-evaluating priorities and swiftly taking suitable action. They can quickly analyze a situation, recalibrate their priorities, and make well-informed decisions to pursue their goals effectively.

BUILDING EFFECTIVE TEAMS

In team building, strong and effective leadership is essential. The team leader may be designated by someone outside the team or selected from within by the team members themselves. The most effective team leaders are often chosen from within, having displayed the ability to foster relationships based on trust and loyalty with the team's members, as opposed to designated leaders who must rely on position and hierarchical power to exercise their leadership initially.

A key element of impactful leadership is the acknowledgment and appreciation of each team member's ideas and contributions. Exceptional leaders are aware that no suggestion is too small or trivial and encourage their team to voice their opinions without fear of criticism or mockery. They cultivate an atmosphere where each member feels acknowledged and valued.

Beyond appreciating ideas, proficient leaders also tune into the unspoken emotions and sentiments of their team members. They lead by example, being open, accessible, and empathetic. Sensitivity to the team's moods and feelings enables leaders to nurture a supportive and empathic workplace.

Another critical role of a team leader is to act as a unifying force. They proactively address and resolve minor conflicts or disagreements within the team. Effective leaders prevent conflicts from escalating by reminding the team of their collective goals and values and refocusing attention on a shared objective.

Communication involves both the transmitter (leader) and receiver (team). Clear and effective communication is the keystone that supports successful leadership. Outstanding leaders recognize the need to convey instructions and directives in a manner that is comprehensible to their team. They must dedicate time to ensuring that any task or project's purpose, expectations, and intended results are explicitly communicated, thus minimizing the chance of confusion or misinterpretation.

The Impact of Leadership on Team Dynamics

The influence you have on your team's emotions is profound and can be either uplifting or detrimental. It's critical for you to have self-awareness to recognize and address any personal blind spots. Moreover, qualities like empathy and an understanding of organizational dynamics are key for you to effectively inspire, influence, manage conflicts, and foster teamwork. Central to achieving this is your genuine concern for and attentive listening to your team members.

Emotional intelligence is vital in driving and shaping team behaviors, correlating directly with team performance. Promoting emotional intelligence within your team improves both their EI and yours, factors that contribute to enhancing team morale and motivation, pushing them to excel and break through barriers. This, in turn, leads to increased productivity, job satisfaction, commitment, and loyalty.

For effective leadership, you need to demonstrate passion, compassion, commitment and dedication. You can inspire and motivate your team members to emulate these qualities. Leadership begins at the top; you must be the catalyst for attracting, developing, and retaining skilled EI individuals in the team.

LEADING WITH EMPATHY

Chapter 4 discussed empathy as a mainstay for Pillar 3 – Social Awareness. Empathy is a vital attribute in leadership. What can empathy do for you as a leader?

Leaders who are empathetic forge robust connections with their team, grasp their deeper needs and motivations, and cultivate a constructive work atmosphere. This sense of empathy allows leaders to engage with team members on a more personal level, enhancing communication, trust, and mutual respect within the team.

Empathetic leaders are adept at conflict resolution and devising solutions that benefit all parties, as they can appreciate the viewpoints of everyone involved. Exhibiting empathy helps nurture a culture of kindness and support, encouraging team members to collaborate effectively towards shared objectives.

Additionally, empathy profoundly influences employee engagement and satisfaction. When team members feel understood and appreciated, their motivation, creativity, and productivity surge, boosting your organization's performance. Empathy enables you to foster a workplace where employees feel valued and supported, leading to higher job satisfaction and better employee retention. Integrating empathy into your leadership approach will create a more positive work environment and drive your organization toward more tremendous success.

What Does Empathy in Leadership Involve?

The concept of co-experience is grounded in empathy, which is fundamentally about understanding and sharing the feelings of another person. Empathy means immersing yourself in another's perspective and experiencing their emotions in a particular situation.

Active listening is a crucial aspect of empathy for you as a leader. It requires paying close attention to what the other person conveys, both through words and non-verbal signals, to show that you fully grasp their point of view.

You must be able to detect emotional signals in others. Non-verbal indicators such as body language, tone of voice, and facial expressions are rich sources of insight into someone's emotional state. These cues are essential for comprehending another's feelings and providing supportive responses.

Empathy also involves a sincere interest in the other person's thoughts, feelings, and life experiences. Demonstrating this interest indicates your commitment to genuinely understanding their perspective. This involves setting aside your own judgments and biases and engaging meaningfully in the conversation.

Are You Expressing Empathy in Leadership?

An employee approaches you because they missed work yesterday due to a sick child and will not make today's deadline on a project. Your automatic response, knowing empathy is important as a leader, pops out, "I'm sorry to hear that. I understand what you are going through." But do you? If you are not a parent yourself, your attempt to empathize might not fully resonate with them, potentially coming off as disingenuous or even condescending.

It's not uncommon for supervisors, managers, and leaders to find themselves in such situations at work. A survey involving over a thousand U.S. employees revealed that 52% perceive their company's attempts at empathy as insincere. This indicates a gap in how empathy is expressed by management and leadership.

For those new to management, this balancing act of building trust and showing genuine concern can be particularly daunting. Your team is observing your every move, making it challenging to express empathy in a way that feels real rather than forced or superficial.

So, what's the solution? Building authentic connections with your team starts with recognizing the essence of the challenge. Why are you getting it wrong even when you are trying to express what is truly heartfelt?

The confusion between sympathy and empathy is common. Sympathy involves feeling sorry for someone's situation because you can personally relate, making statements like, "I feel you," appropriate. However, in today's diverse work environments, you cannot expect to relate to many of the issues employees face personally.

True empathy involves showing compassion and understanding for someone's situation without needing to have experienced it yourself. It means putting yourself in their shoes, acknowledging their feelings, and responding thoughtfully.

Empathy enables you as a leader to form meaningful relationships and trust with your team members, facilitating compassionate interactions regardless of personal experience.

To create a supportive atmosphere where everyone feels valued, you must learn to exhibit genuine empathy. This approach encourages a positive team culture, enhancing productivity, innovation, and job satisfaction (Valadon, 2023).

Here are steps to express empathy more authentically:

1. **Active Listening and Curiosity:** Genuine empathy begins with how you receive and process information shared by your team members. Pay attention to non-verbal cues and listen with the intent to understand, not just respond. Express your willingness to understand their perspective more deeply by asking for more information when appropriate.
2. **Acknowledging Without Assuming Solutions:** Leaders often feel the need to solve problems. However, personal or emotional issues don't always have clear solutions. Sometimes, simply giving space for the employee to speak and feel acknowledged is more impactful.
3. **Avoid Generic Responses:** Empathy isn't one-size-fits-all. Avoid using the same response for every situation. Tailor your reactions to the individual, showing that you've truly listened and understood their unique circumstances.
4. **Making Time for Employees:** Effective leadership involves prioritizing your team. If you're busy when an employee needs to talk, schedule a specific time to discuss their concerns. Showing that you're making time for them reinforces your commitment to their well-being.
5. **Show That You Care:** Responding with compassion and kindness and providing support when necessary fosters a safe and trusting environment where individuals feel at ease sharing their emotions.

Reflecting on your own emotional state is also crucial. Being aware of your own feelings enhances your ability to recognize and empathize with others' emotions and better control your responses. Seeking feedback from team members is important for improving your empathy. Request their views on your empathetic interactions and suggestions for enhancement. This input is invaluable for your continued growth.

Finally, make empathy a consistent practice. Regularly engage in empathetic behavior and conversations, turning empathy into a habit. Continuous practice will help you further develop and strengthen your skills over time (Valadon, 2023).

CHAPTER RECAP

In this chapter, we looked at emotional intelligence in leadership, leadership styles and EI and the importance of adaptability in leadership, along with building teams. We covered leading with empathy and how to determine if you are effectively expressing empathy.

ACTION ITEMS

Emotional intelligence plays a crucial role in adaptability, particularly in showcasing effective leadership skills and guiding individuals in the right direction. When you are emotionally intelligent, you possess a willingness to continuously learn and grow, benefiting both yourself and your ability to lead others. These are a few exercises that can be practiced to enhance your leadership EI skills.

- **Take conscious note of your actions and motivations.** Regularly question why you are engaging in certain activities. Is it for personal gain, to benefit others, or driven by a specific purpose? Reflecting on the intention behind your actions helps you prioritize tasks and gain a better understanding of yourself.
- **Create a list of your daily activities.** Write down the reasons behind each task. This exercise allows you to identify what truly matters and assess whether your time is being allocated efficiently. It helps cultivate focus and self-awareness.
- **Pause when stressed.** When faced with stressful situations, take a step back, close your eyes, and focus on your breath. Consciously experience each inhale and exhale, allowing yourself to monitor your state of mind. By taking this pause, you can avoid immediate reactions and give yourself the opportunity to regain composure. Once you are in a calmer state, you can think more clearly and respond appropriately.

Empathy equips you to establish strong team relationships, handle conflicts efficiently, encourage a compassionate and supportive culture, and enhance employee engagement and satisfaction. Integrating empathy into your leadership approach will create a more positive work environment and drive your organization toward greater success.

Now, let's explore the next chapter on how EI assists in lifelong learning.

CHAPTER 8
EMOTIONAL INTELLIGENCE AND LIFELONG LEARNING

Life's journey is enriched with various experiences, which serve as a foundation for self-discovery and understanding. Personal growth is essential for you and for everyone, yet it is often overlooked. Asking yourself insightful questions is a key method for fostering self-improvement. Notably, well-crafted questions lead to valuable insights,

Here are two meaningful questions to ponder for enhancing personal growth:

1. Which skill do I most need to develop? We all have our strengths and weaknesses, and it's typically our weaknesses that limit our growth and achievement. While nurturing strengths is important, achieving a balanced skill set is equally valuable. Recognizing the skills or areas in need of enhancement can catalyze personal growth and expand one's horizons.
2. Which aspects of my life can I actually influence? Stress often arises from preoccupying oneself with uncontrollable factors. Concentrating on the elements of

life that are within our influence and dedicating time, effort, and thought to these areas is crucial. This question promotes self-awareness and encourages a shift towards more productive and meaningful life areas.

THE LEARNING MINDSET

When embarking on a new job or career journey, it's common to believe that you already have all the skills and knowledge required to excel. However, simply managing daily tasks isn't enough for professional growth or career advancement. Embracing a continuous learning mindset actively seeking educational opportunities, acquiring new skills, and increasing marketability for future roles is crucial. Here are some ways to nurture and sustain this mindset.

Make learning a part of your everyday life: Prioritize learning by incorporating it into your daily agenda. Dedicate a small portion of your day, even just 15 minutes, to activities like reading industry-relevant articles, listening to podcasts, or any other knowledge-enhancing pursuits. Treating it as a concrete task adds a sense of achievement upon completion, which helps reinforce the habit and keeps you motivated to persist.

View your current job as a learning platform: Rather than seeing your role as just fulfilling certain duties, regard it as an opportunity to gain skills and knowledge for your next career step. Employers often value employees who show eagerness to learn beyond their immediate role. If you come across intriguing projects or teams within your organization, show your interest and explore possibilities for involvement. Suggest taking on extra projects that not only help you develop new skills but also align with the company's objectives and ease your manager's workload.

THE GROWTH MINDSET

Adopting a growth mindset means recognizing that your abilities and talents are not static but can be enhanced through dedication, learning, and perseverance. This mindset is characterized by tackling challenges with optimism, viewing failures as opportunities for growth, and consistently adapting and evolving.

In the business realm, fostering your growth mindset is key to achieving success through constantly seeking to improve yourself and your work. You actively engage in learning new skills, trying out varied strategies, and are open to making significant changes in your methods. When confronted with obstacles, you recover quickly, seeing these hurdles as opportunities for both personal and professional development.

Cultivating a growth mindset is beneficial for you throughout your business journey or entrepreneurial endeavors. It marks the difference between just getting by and truly excelling in the dynamic and constantly changing business world. By embracing a growth mindset, you remain adaptable, continuously learn and adjust to new challenges, and seize opportunities for innovation and advancement.

Why is Growth Mindset Important?

Embracing a growth mindset is crucial as it brings several benefits that significantly contribute to both personal and professional advancement. This mindset breeds resilience, leading you to perceive challenges not as hindrances but as opportunities for development. Instead of being demotivated by obstacles, you approach them as avenues for learning, ready to exert the needed effort to overcome them.

Additionally, a growth mindset is key to fostering a culture of continuous learning. You recognize that skills and knowledge can be cultivated through persistent effort and practice. You are receptive to feedback and actively look for chances to broaden your understanding and enhance your capabilities. Such a mindset ensures you are adaptable and flexible, always eager to learn and evolve amidst change.

Furthermore, a growth mindset is a powerful driver of success. By welcoming challenges and maintaining determination in the face of adversity, you boost your prospects of achieving your objectives. You comprehend that success is a result of continued hard work, innovative problem-solving, and learning from failures, not just innate talent. This mindset encourages you to take calculated risks and capitalize on opportunities, leading to greater achievements and personal gratification.

Developing a growth mindset extends beyond a mere shift in thought; it involves actively engaging in behaviors that demonstrate a commitment to ongoing learning and development. This requires moving out of your comfort zone, seeking fresh challenges, and valuing feedback as a tool for growth. By embracing a growth mindset, you begin to see every experience as an opportunity for growth, which influences your actions, responses, and overall approach to various life scenarios.

Strategies for Developing a Growth Mindset

"Whether you think you can, or think you can't – you are right."

HENRY FORD

Cultivating a growth mindset involves consciously altering your beliefs and behaviors. It begins with acknowledging and contesting the notion of a fixed mindset, such as the belief that your capabilities are unchangeable. Instead, you should perceive challenges, weaknesses, and obstacles as opportunities for development and learning.

Embracing challenges is a crucial element of the growth mindset. Instead of shying away from difficulties, you should welcome them as opportunities to expand your abilities, venture beyond your comfort zone, and acquire new skills. Shifting your mindset from "I can't do this" to "I can't do this yet" opens the door to potential growth.

Redefining failure is also integral to a growth mindset. Failure should not be viewed as a finality but as an invaluable lesson. It isn't indicative of your capabilities, but rather a guidepost on the path to success. By evaluating your mistakes, learning from them, and applying these lessons, you can evolve and advance.

Valuing effort is key in nurturing a growth mindset. Growth demands consistent effort and perseverance, even when the pace of progress is slow. Setting specific, effort-based goals and tracking our progress keeps us engaged and driven. Celebrating every effort, big or small, reinforces the concept that abilities can develop through dedication and time.

A relentless desire to learn is the heart of a growth mindset. Approaching each day with curiosity, actively seeking new information, and continuously aiming to better yourself are all vital. Embracing the joy of learning and prioritizing personal development fuels your ongoing growth.

Persistence is essential in a growth mindset. It's about overcoming challenges and not giving in to hardship. Instead of reverting to comfort, you should lean into discomfort, viewing setbacks as growth opportunities. Understanding that significant achievements require time and effort aids in maintaining a healthy perspective and commitment to your growth path.

Being receptive to and acting upon constructive feedback is critical in adopting a growth mindset. Feedback offers invaluable insights, helping identify areas for improvement and blind spots. Actively seeking mentors, coaches, or colleagues for constructive criticism is crucial for your development.

Surrounding yourself with others who share a growth mindset can significantly influence our own development. Their optimism, resilience, and commitment to growth can serve as motivation. Creating a network of supportive individuals who encourage and challenge us is vital for our growth journey.

Finally, learning from others' successes is important. Viewing their achievements as inspiration rather than competition allows us to learn from their methods and adapt them to our own pursuits. Observing and incorporating their strategies enhances our growth experience.

LEARNING FROM EXPERIENCE

Learning through experience, also known as experiential learning, is a method where you gain knowledge and skills by actively participating and engaging in practical activities. This approach emphasizes reflecting on your experiences, identifying newly acquired skills and industry insights, and applying these learnings in a professional context.

Companies, educational institutions, and training bodies often create opportunities for experiential learning, especially for those new to a field or students. These experiences are designed to help you identify your professional strengths, experiment with different roles, and gain hands-on knowledge. Your organization may integrate experiential learning into their recruitment and training strategies, enabling you to find roles that resonate with your interests and skills.

The experiential learning process comprises four key stages:

1. **Concrete Experience:** This stage involves direct participation in practical activities to enhance skills and gain insights. Activities might include executing a specific task, contributing to a project, or partaking in simulation exercises.
2. **Reflective Observation:** Post-experience, you take time to reflect on your learnings. You assess your performance, pinpoint strengths and areas needing improvement, and contemplate the lessons and insights garnered from the activity.
3. **Abstract Conceptualization:** Following reflection, you analyze and interpret the skills and knowledge you have acquired. You explore how these new competencies can be

applied to specific tasks and roles in your professional life and often your personal life.
4. **Active Experimentation:** Equipped with new skills and strategies, you then apply your learning in new situations or tasks to refine your abilities further. This might involve experimenting with various methods, taking on new responsibilities, or embarking on projects that foster ongoing growth and skill application.

Through this cycle, you can maximize the benefits of experiential learning, significantly advancing your professional development and expertise. Experiential learning is vital in bridging the gap between theoretical knowledge and practical application, deepening understanding of your strengths and areas for improvement, and effectively translating these learnings to excel in professional roles.

CONTINUOUS IMPROVEMENT

Continuous improvement is a methodical approach aimed at improving processes through small, gradual modifications over time. It operates on the principle that every process can be refined, as perfection is always an ongoing pursuit. Through regular observation and assessment of existing processes, organizations can pinpoint opportunities to enhance efficiency and reduce waste, resulting in notable improvements.

At the heart of continuous improvement is the persistent quest to refine resources and empower employees to actively participate in boosting the company's performance. This approach transcends a singular improvement initiative, embracing a sustained commitment to incremental changes that lead to significant outcomes.

The central aspects of continuous improvement can be categorized into three main areas:

1. **Upgrade Tools and Materials:** This area focuses on evaluating and upgrading the tools, equipment, and materials used in organizational processes. By adopting improved or newer technologies, organizations can boost efficiency, precision, and overall output.
2. **Develop People and Relationships:** Acknowledging the crucial role of individuals in the process, this focus area aims to elevate success through human resources. Investments in training, skill advancement opportunities, and nurturing a supportive work atmosphere that promotes teamwork and creativity are key. Developing employees' skills and capabilities leads to heightened productivity and fosters a culture of continuous improvement.
3. **Improve the Work Environment:** This aspect involves examining and optimizing the physical workspace, including layout, ergonomic considerations, and safety protocols. Enhancing the work setting can lead to increased employee satisfaction, minimize the likelihood of mistakes or accidents, and encourage overall productivity and well-being.

Focusing on these three key areas enables organizations to effectively propel continuous improvement. Through consistent monitoring and assessment of existing processes, coupled with empowering employees to propose and enact changes, organizations can progressively refine their operations, make the most of their resources, and ultimately boost their financial performance. Embracing continuous improvement represents a long-standing dedication to achieving excellence and is vital for businesses aiming to remain competitive and prosper in the ever-evolving corporate landscape of today.

Benefits of a Continuous Improvement Mindset

A continuous improvement approach can drive the development of a company's products and services by actively seeking ways to enhance processes and deliver more competitive offerings to customers and shareholders.

Implementing a continuous improvement program directly addresses employee engagement. Empowering employees to actively participate in problem-solving and process improvement helps them recognize the value of their ideas and work. This process can lead to increased motivation, more innovative suggestions, and improved productivity within the organization.

One of the key benefits of continuous improvement is eliminating steps that don't add value and improving processes with low value. This approach results in increased efficiency, reducing the time required to complete tasks. By accomplishing more in the same amount of time, the company can benefit from increased productivity and ultimately experience higher profits.

Another intrinsic value of adopting a continuous improvement approach is the identification and resolution of issues and errors in business processes. By focusing on reducing errors and waste through methods like Six Sigma, employees become more proficient in their jobs. This process, in turn, leads to delivering a more robust customer experience and reducing operational inefficiencies and costs.

Implementing a well-planned continuous improvement plan can also have a positive impact on the company's organizational culture. By setting realistic expectations and aligning employee actions with the company's primary goals, employees gain a better understanding of their role. This approach fosters a better working environment, reducing stress, improving teamwork, and increasing overall productivity.

Continuous improvement also leads to improved innovation in developing new products and services, adding more value for customers. Customers perceive companies that continuously improve as offering better results and reliability. This reputation, in turn, positively impacts the company's reputation.

Furthermore, continuous improvement not only results in more efficient processes but also enables companies to find new and better ways of completing tasks. These innovations, even if small, can lead to a significant shift in how the business operates. Companies that continuously innovate in small steps from bottom to top are more likely to outperform their competition.

Organizations that prioritize continuous improvement and have well-defined goals can attract top talent. The opportunity to contribute to the company's success and learn from it becomes an attractive proposition for candidates. This also empowers teams to seek more opportunities for growth and advancement within the organization.

By implementing a continuous improvement approach, companies can also reduce employee turnover. The stability and motivation provided by continuous improvement initiatives lead to cost savings by reducing recruitment, hiring, and training expenses. Employees benefit from a more stable workplace that allows for professional growth.

The ultimate outcome of continuous improvement is a better customer experience. Happier employees, higher quality products and services, and faster delivery times enable companies to build an outstanding brand reputation, improve their market positioning, and achieve a better return on investment. An exceptional customer experience is pivotal to building a successful brand.

CHAPTER RECAP

This chapter covered EI as a lifelong learning concern, examining learning and growth mindsets, experiential learning, and continuous improvement.

These concepts open up virtually limitless possibilities for you. The 4 Pillars of Emotional Intelligence are strengthened in a synergistic fashion. You and your organization become more self-aware and better self-managed. Social awareness drives actions, strategy and policy, which in turn enhances relationship management, for you individually and for your organization as a whole.

ACTION ITEMS

There are various strategies and practices that can aid in regulating our emotions effectively. Here are a few examples:

- **Self-compassion and loving-kindness meditation:** By practicing self-compassion, you can develop a kind and understanding attitude towards yourself. This attitude allows you to acknowledge and accept your emotions without judgment. Loving-kindness meditation involves directing well-wishes and positive thoughts towards yourself and others, fostering emotional balance and well-being.

- **Music meditation:** Dedicating time to listening to calming and relaxing music can help you unwind and soothe your emotions. By immersing yourself in the melodic sounds, you can create a space to reflect and find inner peace.
- **Reminiscence therapy:** This technique can be useful for resolving emotional conflicts involving other people. By deliberately recalling and reflecting on positive memories shared with someone you are currently struggling with, you can evoke feelings of warmth, connection, and understanding, facilitating self-management and reconciliation.
- **Breathing exercises:** Engaging in intentional and focused breathing exercises can promote self-management. Techniques such as breath control, breath counting, and simple breath relaxation can help you calm your mind, regulate your heart rate, and bring a sense of tranquility to your emotions.
- **Simple self-care activities:** Engaging in acts of self-care is vital for self-management. Activities like taking a hot bath, treating yourself to a relaxing massage, or cooking a nourishing meal can provide a sense of comfort and well-being, helping to alleviate stress and temper your emotions.

CHAPTER 9
EMOTIONAL INTELLIGENCE AND MENTAL HEALTH

Emotional intelligence (EI) has emerged as a vital element in management and workplace effectiveness. Beyond its significance in career advancement, EI is equally important for personal resilience in dealing with challenges, stress, trauma, and loss. This chapter explores how EI intersects with mental health and its impact on personal mental well-being.

Those with high emotional intelligence are adept at recognizing their own emotions, empathizing with others, and managing both internal and external stress and conflicts effectively. Developing your EI skills is especially beneficial in maintaining mental and emotional health, whether dealing with job-related stress or personal life traumas.

Mental health is about managing daily life stresses, functioning efficiently, and enriching your own and others' lives. Mental health challenges often stem from difficulties in handling emotions, reactions, and behaviors. Having reliable internal coping mechanisms and access to supportive resources is crucial.

Developed EI skills enable you to identify issues, understand their underlying causes, and address them effectively or seek external support from personal connections or professional counseling. Strengthening your 4 Pillars of EI, particularly self-awareness and self-management, helps control emotions, build resilience, and improve mental health and well-being. This, in turn, enhances social awareness and the management of relationships in challenging situations.

At an organizational level, integrating EI into your work practices enhances mental and social readiness for collaboration, conflict resolution, and communication. This not only leads to more effective teamwork and increased job satisfaction among employees but also reduces burnout. Consequently, it fosters a healthy and sustainable culture within the organization.

EMOTIONAL WELL-BEING

Your emotional well-being, health, and wellness are about your capacity to comprehend, accept, and adeptly handle your emotions. This aspect is crucial in determining how effectively you will manage day-to-day activities, confront challenges, and adapt amidst changes and uncertainties.

With a high degree of emotional well-being, you will be better at dealing with the various highs and lows of life. You can recognize and accept your emotions, whether they are positive or negative, and address them in a constructive and healthy way. This involves regulating emotions, expressing them appropriately, and seeking help or support when necessary.

Conversely, your struggles with emotional well-being can negatively impact both mental and physical health. If you find it challenging to manage your emotions, you may suffer from heightened stress, concentration problems, and reduced capacity to handle everyday challenges. Prolonged difficulties in managing emotions can lead to mental health issues like anxiety or depression, and even physical health problems.

Maintaining emotional well-being is vital for your overall health and functionality. It equips you with the resilience to overcome life's hurdles, make thoughtful decisions, sustain healthy relationships, and cope with stress effectively. By focusing on improving your emotional well-being, you will enhance your life quality and achieve greater happiness and fulfillment.

EMOTIONAL INTELLIGENCE AND MENTAL HEALTH

Self-awareness, Pillar 1, is a crucial element of emotional intelligence. It gives you the insight to identify and comprehend various facets of your personality, including your emotions and feelings. Rather than being controlled by your emotions, you approach self-reflection with confidence and honesty. An honest look at your strengths and weaknesses empowers you to seek help when needed, give help when asked, and make well-informed decisions.

When you excel at self-management, Pillar 2, you are not easily swayed by negative emotions such as anger or jealousy. You intentionally take a moment to reflect before acting, which helps you avoid rash decisions and thoughtless errors. You manage your emotions and responses without impulse, with purpose and effectiveness.

Your high EI in social awareness, Pillar 3, proves invaluable in team settings. You excel as an attentive listener and effective communicator. Your empathy allows you to understand others' emotions. You are driven to self-improve and succeed, proactive in initiating and leading positive changes.

Your relationship management, Pillar 4, is strong. You are adept at managing conflicts and proficient in building relationships. You readily embrace new challenges and are keen to develop the necessary skills to excel in diverse scenarios.

Emotion Regulation and Mental Health

Recognizing and naming your emotions is a crucial strategy in emotion regulation. Primary emotions are your instinctive responses to external events, like feeling sadness after the loss of a loved one or anger in response to mistreatment. Secondary emotions are not instinctive but rather your response or reaction to the primary emotions. They are within your control, such as frustration from dwelling on an issue, anxiety over things you cannot control, or lashing out at others when you are upset.

Learning to accept your primary emotions without self-criticism is an important skill. This involves understanding, identifying, and labeling your emotions, laying a groundwork for effectively managing your secondary emotional reactions. Labeling your emotions for what they are and accepting them helps prevent you from falling into a cycle of negative emotions and thoughts, which could lead to unhelpful, unhealthy behaviors, which cycle back into negative emotions and thoughts.

You must learn to accept and release negative feelings to handle your emotions more effectively. Rather than clinging to these emotions or fixating on them, it's healthier to confront them directly and understand that they are natural reactions to your situation and surroundings.

Accepting your own suffering can be challenging, but it's a step towards healthier emotional well-being. Acceptance encourages you to face difficult emotions instead of avoiding them. Often, you may discover that these emotions are not as daunting as you anticipated and are more manageable than you initially thought.

Mindfulness and Mental Health

Mindfulness is a state of being fully immersed in the present moment, marked by acute awareness and acceptance of your thoughts, feelings, and environment without any judgment. Research indicates that practicing mindfulness leads to numerous benefits, such as decreased stress, improved mental health, and overall better well-being.

The link between mindfulness and emotional intelligence lies in the development of self-awareness. To be emotionally intelligent, one needs to be conscious of their own emotions and those of others. Mindfulness enhances this self-awareness, guiding individuals to observe their thoughts and feelings neutrally, free from bias or judgment. This level of self-awareness is crucial in emotional intelligence, as it allows individuals to accurately identify their emotions, their triggers, and the potential effects on their behavior.

Moreover, mindfulness is instrumental in emotion regulation. It equips individuals with skills to effectively manage their thoughts and feelings, preventing them from being overwhelmed by them. This ability to control one's emotions is a vital component of emotional intelligence, aiding in stress management, overcoming challenges, and fostering stronger relationships.

Lastly, mindfulness significantly improves communication and interpersonal relationships. Regular mindfulness practice increases an individual's ability to stay focused on the present, enhancing interactions with others. This heightened presence improves active listening and understanding of others' emotions, fostering empathy and responsiveness. Consequently, this leads to more effective communication and deeper, more meaningful relationships.

MANAGING STRESS AND ANXIETY

Your developed emotional intelligence will build several distinctive traits and behaviors that contribute significantly to your success and well-being, managing your stress and mitigating your anxiety.

1. Your high EI allows you a clear vision of your life goals, your WHY or Deep Purpose, and the steps needed to actively work towards achieving them, your HOW or Deep Goals. You understand your motivations and values well, which guides you in finding this WHY and HOW; your purpose, meaning, and direction in life to bring you delight and satisfaction from your endeavors.
2. You will excel in recognizing and articulating your emotions. Your profound insight into your emotional states enables you to manage your reactions to different situations effectively. This self-awareness, openness, and assertiveness help you address the underlying causes of your emotions, not just the symptoms.
3. Another key trait is your ability to stay composed in challenging situations. You can manage your emotional reactions by identifying and accepting your feelings, helping you remain calm when others might be overwhelmed.
4. Additionally, you are skilled at interpreting their emotions. You analyze the significance of each emotion and adjust your responses accordingly, ensuring you are appropriate

and constructive. This skill involves discerning which emotions to nurture and which to reevaluate or reframe.

This awareness and understanding make you adept at reducing anxiety during stressful periods. By understanding stress triggers and recognizing stress indicators, you can reinterpret stressful events and take effective actions, including self-advocacy, thus maintaining control in tough situations.

With developed EI, you will shine in your interpersonal relationships. You are an attentive listener, empathize with others, and can interpret non-verbal cues like tone, facial expressions, and body language, leading to swift, effective responses that build trust and authentic connections. You are open to learning from mistakes and welcoming criticism. They seek feedback and are not deterred by negative comments, using them constructively for personal growth.

You listen to your inner voice, prioritizing your true desires and values over societal expectations or ego-driven impulses. You understand the importance of asking for help. You know this is a strength and a means to collaborate and leverage others' expertise. You are mindful of your impact on others. You practice pausing and reflecting on your actions and words, emphasizing empathy and compassionate accountability.

You shift from making assumptions to being curious. You avoid taking things personally, embracing a growth mindset focused on continuous learning and development. You avoid passing judgment hastily, choosing instead to approach situations with curiosity and seek understanding, seeing challenges as opportunities for growth and transformation. You focus on what you can control, directing your energy and efforts to areas where they can make a significant impact, rather than fixating on uncontrollable aspects.

> *"Lord, grant me the* Serenity *to accept the things I cannot change, the* Courage *to change the things I can, and the* Wisdom *to know the difference."*
>
> AA SERENITY PRAYER

CHAPTER RECAP

You possess a spectrum of skills and attributes that bolster both your personal and professional lives. Your ability to understand and manage emotions, forge strong relationships, and focus on personal growth enables you to tackle challenges resiliently and achieve your objectives.

In this chapter, we examined emotional intelligence, emotion regulation, and mindfulness as they relate to emotional well-being and mental health. Your developed EI will help maintain balance in these two primary areas: managing stress and mitigating anxiety.

ACTION ITEMS

To better handle negative emotions, there are steps you can follow to work on your ability to let them go.

- Begin by observing your emotions, acknowledging that they exist, and standing back to detach yourself from them. Journal about the negative emotions you have felt

today, how you handled them, and how you would like to handle them in the future.
- As you do this work, try to experience your emotions as waves that come and go. It may be helpful to focus on certain aspects of the emotion, such as how your body is physically responding or any imagery that comes to mind. Recognize that although your emotion is a part of you, it does not define your whole being.
- In addition, it is not always necessary to act on your emotions. Just because you are feeling a certain way does not mean that you must do something about it. Sometimes, simply sitting with the emotion and letting it pass is the best course of action. Acting impulsively can often intensify and prolong negative emotions.

It is important to observe your emotions, recognize that you are not solely defined by them, and avoid making impulsive decisions based solely on them. Instead, try to experience them without judgment and let them pass naturally. By practicing these steps, you can learn how to let go of negative emotions more effectively.

CHAPTER 10
EMOTIONAL INTELLIGENCE AND TRANSFORMATION

"Mastering others is strength; mastering yourself is true power."

LAO TZU

Many people tend to focus on their strengths while neglecting their weaknesses. However, top achievers like superstars, masters, and elite performers adopt different strategies. They proactively address their weaknesses and seek breakthroughs in those areas, a key factor in their journey to excellence. This method is not exclusive to them; anyone can embark on this path to greatness.

Self-limiting beliefs hold us back and breed complacency, doubt, and fear, which in turn lead to stagnation, stress, and unhappiness. The path to self-mastery involves an internal transformation. By pressing out against your limitations, affirming your actions, and shedding your fears, you will enhance your personal presence, achieve peace of mind, and increase your overall happiness.

To truly reach your fullest potential and foster personal growth, it's crucial to acknowledge and work on your weaknesses. This effort helps you break free from self-imposed constraints, dispel fears and doubts, and ultimately attain inner peace and joy. Pursuing self-mastery is a profound, life-changing, and continuing life-long journey that can positively influence all facets of your life.

TRANSFORMING LIFE AND LEADERSHIP

The relationship between transformational leadership and emotional intelligence has long been a topic of research interest. EI encompasses the emotional and social skills that shape how we perceive and express ourselves, how we develop and maintain relationships, and how we utilize emotional information to temper our decisions. Transformational leadership refers to certain traits and behaviors exhibited by leaders that directly connect with these constructs of being highly emotionally intelligent.

The Transformative Power of EI

As you learn and become aware of triggers and behaviors, you can begin controlling your impulses and managing your actions in different situations. Become aware of your emotions and reactions and make conscious choices about how you will respond. A very important aspect of self-regulation is controlling your anger and not lashing out, understanding that such a reaction will only create more problems. Instead, take a moment to reflect on what is happening and consider the dynamics of the conflict.

To improve your self-awareness, adopt and align with these practices we covered earlier:

- **Actively listening:** By truly paying attention to others and being present in conversations, you can understand different perspectives and develop empathy. This practice also allows you to better understand yourself and your reactions.
- **Practicing mindfulness and consciousness:** Mindfulness involves being fully present in the moment and non-judgmentally observing your thoughts and emotions. This ability helps you to become more aware of your own internal experiences and enables you to respond proactively rather than react impulsively.
- **Developing a growth mindset:** Cultivating a belief in your ability to learn and grow allows you to approach challenges with a positive attitude. This mindset encourages self-reflection and a willingness to adapt and improve.
- **Keeping a journal:** Writing down your thoughts and feelings can help you explore and understand yourself on a deeper level. It provides an opportunity for self-reflection and can reveal patterns or triggers that may impact your behaviors.
- **Practicing gratitude:** Focusing on what you are grateful for can shift your mindset towards positivity and enhance your self-awareness. By acknowledging and appreciating the good things in your life, you develop a more balanced perspective.

By incorporating these habits into your daily lives, you gain a deeper understanding of yourself. This helps you navigate conflicts with a clearer perspective and make intentional choices in your behaviors and responses. This, in turn, allows you to engage in healthier and more meaningful relationships.

Here again are some techniques for self-management and regulating emotions:

- **Identifying and mitigating triggers:** It is essential to recognize patterns that lead to intense emotions. Understanding the root causes, such as underlying insecurities or past experiences, allows for effectively managing these triggers.
- **Being mindful of physical symptoms:** Awareness of physical states like hunger or fatigue is important, as they can intensify emotions. Addressing these physical conditions can help reduce the intensity of the emotional response.
- **Practicing positive self-talk:** It's important to avoid negative self-talk in moments of overwhelming emotions. Adopting a self-compassionate and empathetic approach can transform negative thoughts into positive affirmations, helping to lessen the impact of challenging emotions.

SELF-MASTERY AND EMOTIONAL INTELLIGENCE

People often place blame on others when faced with challenges and obstacles in both their personal and professional lives. However, true personal empowerment and success come from taking responsibility for our actions. This is not about self-blame but rather about recognizing the transformative growth that occurs when we focus on improving our attitudes, thoughts, perceptions, feelings, and habits.

Through self-mastery, you gain more control of your life. Set realistic goals and have the confidence and determination to achieve them. Take ownership of your bad habits and weaknesses to make progress toward becoming the best version of yourself. By developing your own self-mastery, you gain insight into understanding and empathizing with others. This allows you to effectively communicate and create genuine connections with others, fostering collaboration and accomplishment for yourself, your colleagues, and your team.

By embracing personal responsibility and committing to self-improvement, you unlock the door to personal empowerment and success. Taking responsibility for your growth and development leads the way to self-mastery and has a positive impact on those around you.

Cultivate your emotional resilience. When you, as a leader, can regulate your emotions and reactions, it creates a safe space for vulnerability within the team. They will feel more comfortable addressing their concerns and opening up to you.

In review, here are a few approaches to self-management by enhancing your resilience:

1. **Establish boundaries and be assertive.** Refusing unreasonable demands and safeguarding your time and energy are crucial aspects of building resilience. Hone your skills in self-advocacy, such as requesting what you need and setting clear boundaries.
2. **Embrace acceptance.** Recognizing that stress, discomfort, and change are inevitable parts of life is a key step in fostering resilience. Understand that your thoughts, emotions, and experiences are legitimate and that you can endure by taking proper care of yourself. Reflecting on what aspects of your life you can and cannot control can be enlightening.
3. **Cultivate connections.** Forming strong, supportive bonds with friends, family, or a therapist is a cornerstone of

emotional resilience. Being open to seeking and receiving necessary support can provide perspective and enhance your mood.
4. **Seek balance.** Striking a healthy balance between work, relaxation, and leisure activities is vital for sustaining emotional resilience. Make your well-being a priority and plan for activities that bring you happiness. Establishing a routine and dedicating time to self-care are important practices to remain anchored during tough periods.

ACHIEVING BALANCE AND HARMONY

Numerous studies have demonstrated the significant role of emotional intelligence in achieving work-life balance. Renowned psychologist Daniel Goleman emphasizes that emotional intelligence is a crucial component of mental aptitude for work-life balance and overall life success. EI empowers employees to leverage their creativity and embrace imaginative problem-solving techniques.

Managing your emotions and handling your reactions to stress are key factors in achieving a healthy work-life balance. Understand your emotions and know how and when to express them. This heightened self-awareness and self-management will equip you to navigate the demands of your jobs and personal responsibilities more easily. You will better adapt to and empathize with others' emotions, establishing you as an effective leader who promotes inclusivity and supportive relationships. As a result, both you and your team will experience higher job satisfaction and overall well-being.

CHAPTER RECAP

In this chapter, we covered emotional intelligence and transformation, transforming your life and leadership through self-mastery and the transformative power of EI to achieve balance and harmony for you and others in the home and at the workplace.

ACTION ITEMS

You can provide significant advantages in the workplace, such as the ability to recognize and interpret nonverbal cues, adapt behavior to different colleagues and situations, make sound decisions, and achieve respected leadership.

Several exercises can enhance your emotional intelligence and that of the people you work with. Conduct a 360-degree assessment, seeking feedback from colleagues, peers, and superiors while also performing your own self-assessment. This practice offers valuable insights into the perceptions of others regarding one's strengths and limits, helping to uncover any blind spots you may not notice yet are important to others.

- For your Get A Grip 360 Assessment ©, email me at KennyLeeBooks@gmail.com with Get A Grip 360 in the Subject line.

Active listening plays an important role in transformative life and leadership. By focusing on the speaker and exhibiting engagement through non-verbal cues, such as paraphrasing or nodding, you can better connect with others and gain a deeper understanding of their thoughts and emotions.

- Over the next week, journal about different times you engaged in active listening. What did you do to promote and communicate that you were actively listening? What non-verbal cues did you consciously use to connect with the person?

For individuals interested in developing their EI skills further, enrolling in an online leadership course or training program may be a beneficial next step. The approach empowers individuals to improve their leadership abilities, effectively motivate and coach teams, enhance communication, and increase productivity and overall morale.

- The company edX For Business has several online courses, some free and some for a fee. Go to: https://www.edx.org/learn/leadership

CONCLUSION

EI is an essential skill for developing and maintaining interpersonal relationships in both your personal and professional lives. Within the workplace and at home, your EI is built upon four pillars: Pillar 1 – Self-Awareness, Pillar 2 – Self-Management, Pillar 3 – Social Awareness, and Pillar 4 – Relationship Management.

EI helps nurture genuine connections, fosters a positive home and work environment, and enables you to inspire and empower your family, friends, and work teams. By incorporating EI into decision-making processes, you can make well-rounded choices that consider the emotions and needs of others. EI equips you with resilience and coping mechanisms to navigate challenges and maintain a positive mindset through all aspects of your life.

Achieving self-mastery puts you in the driver's seat of your life; the possibilities for you are literally endless. Your relationships at home and in the workplace become more cohesive, fulfilling, and synergistic.

Consider this story to wrap things up. In a field just up the road, there are two horses. They both look like any other horses. If you listen closely, you can hear a bell ringing from the field.

However, upon closer inspection, you will notice something remarkable—one of the horses is blind. The bell you hear is attached to the other, smaller horse's halter and signals the blind horse where to find his companion.

As you observe these two friends, you will see that the horse with the bell is always checking on his blind friend, who will listen for the bell ringing and cautiously make his way toward his companion while trusting he is not being led astray. In the evenings, when the horse with the bell returns to the barn, he occasionally turns back to ensure that his blind friend is following him home.

Reflecting on this story, think about your personal and professional life. You have probably experienced times when you felt like the blind horse—in need of inspiration and motivation to realize your full potential. Additionally, there may have been instances when you were like the horse with the bell—providing motivation and inspiration to guide others towards achieving their goals. Both rely on each other to be more than they can be alone.

This story illustrates the importance of mutual support, empathy, and motivation in a relationship. Happiness is not solely based on doing what you enjoy but also on your positive impact on others. It reminds you to appreciate the role you play in motivating and inspiring others, as well as being open to receiving encouragement when you need it.

I hope this book helped you get a grip on your emotional intelligence. It's only a matter of time before you master your emotions and stay in control, building healthy, lasting relationships. It's all about practice and perseverance.

Your Life. Your Health. Your Journey... Take Action!

* * *

Keeping the Game Alive

Now that you're on your way to mastering your emotions, it's your turn to help others find their path to awesomeness.

By sharing your thoughts about this book on Amazon, you're not just leaving a review; you're guiding other friends to where they can discover how to be excellent at handling their feelings, just like you.

A big, giant thank you for helping out. Sharing our knowledge keeps the awesomeness alive, and thanks to you, we're spreading the good vibes far and wide.

Just click on the link below or scan the QR code here:

[https://www.amazon.com/review/review-your-purchases/?asin=B0CZ7V6QCD]

Remember, every bit of kindness you share makes the world a brighter place. Thanks for being part of our mission to spread happiness and smarts all over the place!

Thank you, and bon voyage!

Your Life. Your Health. Your Journey... Take Action!

~ Kenny Lee

P.S. Don't forget!... BONUS exercises to help you Get A Grip On Your Emotional Intelligence are available to you FREE.

Send me an email at:

KennyLeeBooks@gmail.com

and I will send you a bonus set of exercises along with updates as you progress on your Emotional Intelligence journey. Watch for more books in the future.

APPENDIX 1 – GET-A-GRIP EMOTIONAL INTELLIGENCE ASSESSMENT ©

The Get-A-Grip EQ Test is designed to give you a baseline look at your emotional intelligence and then repeated later to show your progress in your journey. Take this test as you start through this book and note your answers and scores in your notebook. After completing the book and the Action Items in each of the chapters, retake the test... without looking at your previous answers :-). Then, look at your previous assessment, compare, and note the changes you have observed in yourself and your perspective of your relationships with others. You can also retake the assessment every 3 months or so to note your progress as you put your learning into practice.

Each statement below will be acknowledged at the following frequencies, which indicate how often it applies to you: Never, Rarely, Sometimes, Usually, Almost Always, and Always.

To score the assessment, use the table that follows the Get-A-Grip EI Assessment © in Appendix 1. Some items have "reverse" scoring, so compare the values for your answers to each individual question.

Let's begin.

The Get-A-Grip EI Assessment ©

	Never	Rarely	Sometimes	Usually	Almost Always	Always
1. I am confident in my capabilities						
2. I acknowledge areas where I need improvement; my weaknesses and shortcomings						
3. I am aware of and understand my emotions as they occur						
4. I am reliable and can be counted on						
5. I accept and adapt to changes that develop						
6. I cope effectively with stress						
7. I play a part in creating my own difficult situations and circumstances						
8. I recognize how my mood and behavior influence and impact others						
9. I notice when others are affecting my emotions and behaviors						
10. I face frustration without getting agitated or upset						
11. I consider many of the options available before making a decision						
12. I disregard and block out others when I get upset at something						
13. I recognize other people's feelings						
14. I am able to read the mood in the group						

	Never	Rarely	Sometimes	Usually	Almost Always	Always
15. I am able to hear what others are trying to say and really mean						
16. I try to find value in all kinds of situations, positive or negative						
17. I refrain from speaking or acting if it will not help the current situation						
18. I act in ways I later regret when I am upset						
19. I am open to feedback and accept constructive criticism						
20. I am reserved and withdrawn in some social situations						
21. I have trouble confronting and talking directly to people in difficult situations						
22. I appreciate and get along well with others						
23. I handle conflicts effectively						
24. I am aware of and sensitive to the feelings of others in my interactions						
25. I make efforts to learn about others to know and get along with them						
26. I clarify and explain my thoughts and feelings to others						
27. I communicate with others effectively						
28. I show others how I care about them and what they are going through						
29. I get defensive when someone critiques or criticizes me						

	Never	Rarely	Sometimes	Usually	Almost Always	Always
30. I wake up ready for the day with a positive attitude						
31. I stay calm and composed when under pressure						
32. I feel stressed when tasks and deadlines need attending to						
33. In meetings, I prioritize my thoughts over listening to others						
34. I feel timid and shy when meeting new people						
35. I easily initiate conversation with others						
36. I express emotions appropriately						
37. I let others know my opinion, especially if I disagree with theirs						
38. I don't care what other people think of me						
39. I always tell the truth when asked for my opinion						
40. I don't let the emotions of others affect me much						
41. I have strong interpersonal skills						
42. I am bothered by others in pain						
43. I emotionally involve myself with the problems of others						
44. I keep my personal problems out of my workplace						

	Never	Rarely	Sometimes	Usually	Almost Always	Always
45. I express my emotions appropriately in the workplace						
46. I set and strive to achieve my goals						
47. I achieve goals with persistence, even if other factors work against me						
48. I like to help others						
49. I like being the center of attention						
50. I believe in my abilities and myself						

Get-A-Grip EI Assessment © Scoring and Action Items

The following is a grid to compare to your answers to obtain your Get-A-Grip EQ Score. This score is not for diagnostic, psychiatric, or psychological assessment. It is a picture of where you stand with yourself on your EQ and is meant to help you Get A Grip On YOUR Emotional Intelligence.

The scoring is from zero (0) to five(5) for most of the items because "Always" doing that particular behavior or having that emotion is a positive and scores a five (5) for your EI. Notice that some items are scored the opposite way, with "Never" equal to five (5) and "Always" equal to zero (0) due to the way the statement is worded.

	Never	Rarely	Sometimes	Usually	Almost Always	Always	MY SCORE
1. I am confident in my capabilities	0	1	2	3	4	5	
2. I acknowledge areas where I need improvement; my weaknesses and shortcomings	0	1	2	3	4	5	
3. I am aware of and understand my emotions as they occur	0	1	2	3	4	5	
4. I am reliable and can be counted on	0	1	2	3	4	5	
5. I accept and adapt to changes that develop	0	1	2	3	4	5	
6. I cope effectively with stress	0	1	2	3	4	5	
7. I play a part in creating my own difficult situations and circumstances	0	1	2	3	4	5	
8. I recognize how my mood and behavior influence and impact others	0	1	2	3	4	5	
9. I notice when others are affecting my emotions and behaviors	0	1	2	3	4	5	
10. I face frustration without getting agitated or upset	0	1	2	3	4	5	

	Never	Rarely	Sometimes	Usually	Almost Always	Always	**MY SCORE**
11. I consider many of the options available before making a decision	0	1	2	3	4	5	
12. I disregard and block out others when I get upset at something	5	4	3	2	1	0	
13. I recognize other people's feelings	0	1	2	3	4	5	
14. I am able to read the mood in the group	0	1	2	3	4	5	
15. I am able to hear what others are trying to say and really mean	0	1	2	3	4	5	
16. I try to find value in all kinds of situations, positive or negative	0	1	2	3	4	5	
17. I refrain from speaking or acting if it will not help the current situation	0	1	2	3	4	5	
18. I act in ways I later regret when I am upset	5	4	3	2	1	0	
19. I am open to feedback and accept constructive criticism	0	1	2	3	4	5	
20. I am reserved and withdrawn in some social situations	5	4	3	2	1	0	
21. I have trouble confronting and talking directly to people in difficult situations	5	4	3	2	1	0	
22. I appreciate and get along well with others	0	1	2	3	4	5	
23. I handle conflicts effectively	0	1	2	3	4	5	
24. I am aware of and sensitive to the feelings of others in my interactions	0	1	2	3	4	5	
25. I make efforts to learn about others to know and get along with them	0	1	2	3	4	5	

	Never	Rarely	Sometimes	Usually	Almost Always	Always	**MY SCORE**
26. I clarify and explain my thoughts and feelings to others	0	1	2	3	4	5	
27. I communicate with others effectively	0	1	2	3	4	5	
28. I show others how I care about them and what they are going through	0	1	2	3	4	5	
29. I get defensive when someone critiques or criticizes me	5	4	3	2	1	0	
30. I wake up ready for the day with a positive attitude	0	1	2	3	4	5	
31. I stay calm and composed when under pressure	0	1	2	3	4	5	
32. I feel stressed when tasks and deadlines need attending to	5	4	3	2	1	0	
33. In meetings, I prioritize my thoughts over listening to others	5	4	3	2	1	0	
34. I feel timid and shy when meeting new people	5	4	3	2	1	0	
35. I easily initiate conversations with others	0	1	2	3	4	5	
36. I express emotions appropriately	0	1	2	3	4	5	
37. I let others know my opinion, especially if I disagree with theirs	5	4	3	2	1	0	
38. I care what other people think of me	0	1	2	3	4	5	
39. I always tell the truth when asked for my opinion	0	1	2	3	4	5	
40. I don't let the emotions of others affect me much	5	4	3	2	1	0	
41. I have strong interpersonal skills	0	1	2	3	4	5	

	Never	Rarely	Sometimes	Usually	Almost Always	Always	MY SCORE
42. I am bothered by others in pain	0	1	2	3	4	5	
43. I emotionally involve myself with the problems of others	0	1	2	3	4	5	
44. I keep my personal problems out of my workplace	0	1	2	3	4	5	
45. I express my emotions appropriately in the workplace	0	1	2	3	4	5	
46. I set and strive to achieve my goals	0	1	2	3	4	5	
47. I achieve goals with persistence, even if other factors work against me	0	1	2	3	4	5	
48. I like to help others	0	1	2	3	4	5	
49. I like being the center of attention	5	4	3	2	1	0	
50. I believe in my abilities and myself	0	1	2	3	4	5	

Total up your scores. Reviewing your test, have you been completely honest with yourself? Do you "Always" do that one thing and "Never" do the other? You took this test to build primarily on Pillar 1 – Self-Awareness and your foundation for the other pillars of EI. Above all, be honest with yourself.

Reference your score and what it means for you. Follow the EI development plan below to help you get a grip on your EI.

Your Score	What Your Score Means For You
225 – 250	STRENGTH IS ON YOUR SIDE You have a solid grip on your Emotional Intelligence. Your scores are much higher than average. It is time now to grab onto the opportunities life offers you and use your emotional intelligence to maximize your successes. You are competent. Set meaningful goals and strive to achieve what you want from life. You have what it takes.

200 – 224	**STRENGTH YOU CAN BUILD ON** You have a basic handle on your Emotional Intelligence. Your scores are above average, but some areas could use some tweaking. Study those areas, journal your results, and follow the plan below.
175 – 199	**A GOOD FOUNDATION FOR IMPROVEMENT** Your awareness is present, and you are doing well in some areas, but other EI behaviors are holding you back. With a little effort, you will see large improvements. Focus on areas where you scored 3 or less and open yourself up to improvements using the plan below. Be methodical and intentional in your journey
150 – 174	**BUILD UP YOUR FOUNDATION** Your EI is not where you need it to be. Pick the things that are most important to you and work on them. There are often things that don't come naturally to you. You must develop those areas. Build up strength in each of your 4 Pillars. You don't want to let others down. You don't want to let yourself down. Pick just one area to start on. Journal your results. As you see improvements, pick another area. Follow the plan below.
149 and below	**START WITH THE BASICS.** Your EI is low, you need to develop it, reaching deep within yourself. Journal your thoughts and progress for the next 6 weeks. • Start with Pillar 1 – Self-Awareness. Work on it for 3 weeks. As you develop self-awareness, your Pillar 2 – Self-management – will progress. • After 3 weeks, include Pillar 3 – Social Awareness – into your work and practice those concepts to develop that along with Pillar 4 – Relationship Management. • At the end of 6 weeks, retake the Get-A-Grip EQ Test to define your progress and lead you to your next step.

EMOTIONAL INTELLIGENCE DEVELOPMENT PLAN

After tallying up your results each time you take the assessment:

- Journal your results. Note the date you took this evaluation and record your scores and your thoughts on how you did.
- Reference and note the areas where you can improve.

Once you complete the book and retake the test for comparison:

- Pick two areas for improvement and focus on them for the coming week.
- Write about your improvements in these two areas and, then…

- Pick two other areas for the following week and repeat the journaling entries.

Every 90 days or so, retake the test and compare your answers to the previous results. Note areas for improvement again and then focus on the areas where you have seen only slight improvement or would like to see more. Consider the following:

- How do you feel about your grip on your emotional intelligence at this point?
- Pillar 1 – Has your self-awareness improved? Do you need to do more in this foundational area? How will you make these improvements happen?
- Pillar 2 – Is your self-management where it needs to be? What items would you like to improve on? What areas do others see as ways you might improve?
- Pillar 3 – Has your social awareness improved? What do others say about it? What social situations can you put yourself in to foster more improvement?
- Pillar 4 – How are your relationships? Think of the 5 people closest to you… how has your relationship improved with each of them? What relationship needs your attention the most?

Next step… BONUS exercises to help you Get a Grip on Your Emotional Intelligence© are available to you FREE.

Send me an email at:

KennyLeeBooks@gmail.com

and I will send you a bonus set of exercises along with updates for your Emotional Intelligence journey into the future.

To your EI and emotional health!

Your Life. Your Health. Your Journey... Take Action!

~ Kenny Lee

APPENDIX 2 – MANAGEMENT OF ANXIETY, ANGER, SADNESS, AND DEPRESSION

* * *

This information is not intended to provide a medical diagnosis or suggested treatments for clinical depression and cannot take the place of seeing a mental health professional.

Contact the 988 Suicide & Crisis Lifeline. Call or text 988 or chat 988lifeline.org if you or someone you know is struggling or in crisis. Help is available.

* * *

ANXIETY, AND STRATEGIES TO MANAGE ANXIETY

Anxiety manifests in various forms, leading to the categorization of different anxiety disorders. Each type has its own unique Cognitive Behavioral Therapy (CBT) treatment strategy, emphasizing the adaptability and effectiveness of CBT in addressing anxiety issues. Compelling evidence supports CBT as the leading method for treating anxiety conditions. Some different types of anxiety disorders include:

- **Social Anxiety Disorder, or Social Phobia:** Involves intense worry over being judged negatively by others. This condition can trigger fear of public speaking, unease in

social gatherings or simple conversations, or a pervasive concern about being scrutinized.
- **Obsessive-Compulsive Disorder (OCD):** Characterized by persistent, unwanted thoughts that cause distress or discomfort, often leading to compulsive behaviors aimed at mitigating anxiety. Although OCD shares similarities with other anxiety disorders, it is classified separately. It's commonly mistaken for Obsessive-Compulsive Personality Disorder, which focuses on extreme perfectionism and control but isn't rooted in anxiety.
- **Panic Attacks:** Acute bouts of anxiety featuring symptoms like rapid heartbeat, sweating, and dizziness. While not inherently dangerous, they can cultivate a fear of these symptoms escalating into Panic Disorder. This can result in avoidance behaviors and increased panic episodes.
- **Posttraumatic Stress Disorder (PTSD):** Anxiety response to traumatic events, marked by recurring distressing memories, avoidance of trauma reminders, and heightened negative emotions.
- **Phobias:** Intense, irrational fears of specific objects or situations, causing significant distress when faced with the feared entity.
- **Generalized Anxiety Disorder:** Involves persistent, uncontrollable worry over various aspects of life, leading to constant anxiety and stress.

Cognitive Behavioral Treatments for anxiety disorders prove highly effective, with over 70% of individuals experiencing notable symptom relief after undergoing 10-20 sessions of therapy. Although specific CBT approaches vary, they share common techniques aimed at combating anxiety.

Anxiety treatment techniques you can use outside of clinical therapy include:

- **Cognitive reassessment and thought evaluation:** This process involves identifying and challenging unhelpful thought patterns for anxiety, helping individuals adopt a more rational and balanced viewpoint, thereby easing anxiety rooted in misconceived fears or exaggerated worries.
- **Techniques for relaxation:** This strategy teaches techniques to ease physical and mental strain, fostering tranquility. Practices may encompass deep breathing, muscle relaxation, and visualization exercises, which aid in lowering overall anxiety and enhancing stress management.
- **Mindfulness practices:** These practices encourage a nonjudgmental awareness of the present. They utilize meditation, breathing exercises, or body scans to observe thoughts and feelings calmly, helping to interrupt anxious thought cycles and promote equilibrium.
- **Addressing insomnia:** In anxiety-focused treatment, improving sleep quality is vital. Strategies include educating on sleep hygiene, establishing consistent sleep patterns, and tackling sleep-related issues, as good sleep hygiene is essential for reducing anxiety and enhancing mental health.
- **Exposure Therapy:** This method involves gradually and systematically facing fears, demonstrating that the feared consequences are often unfounded, thus diminishing anxiety over time. It is particularly beneficial for phobias and specific anxiety triggers.
- **Acceptance training:** This aspect teaches the recognition and acceptance of challenging thoughts and feelings,

understanding that discomfort is part of life, and developing strategies to manage difficult emotions, build resilience, and reduce anxiety.
- **Training in problem-solving:** This training offers structured methods to tackle life's challenges, helping individuals identify issues, brainstorm solutions, and assess their efficacy, thereby improving coping skills and reducing overwhelm-induced anxiety.
- **Additional therapy-based strategies:** CBT may include various other tailored interventions, such as assertiveness training, enhancing social skills, and cognitive restructuring. These allow for a customized treatment plan that addresses unique anxiety triggers and encourages positive changes in thoughts and behaviors.

ANGER, AND ANGER MANAGEMENT

Anger is a familiar emotion to all of us, manifesting in moments of irritation up to periods of intense fury. It's a natural and often beneficial feeling. However, when anger spirals out of control and becomes destructive, it can wreak havoc—disrupting your work life, personal relationships, and the overall quality of your existence. It can leave you feeling like you're at the whim of a formidable, erratic force.

Anger management is designed to help you regulate and mitigate your anger by concentrating on the present and addressing only the problems that require attention. Techniques for managing anger include cognitive behavioral problem-solving, mindfulness training, and the modification of maladaptive thought patterns.

Problem-solving training is particularly beneficial for individuals overwhelmed by seemingly insurmountable issues. This strategy involves identifying the problem, brainstorming potential solutions without immediate judgment, evaluating and selecting a solution, outlining the necessary steps for implementation, learning cognitive techniques for effective execution, and finally, putting the plan into action.

Techniques may be employed to pinpoint and adjust maladaptive thought patterns. Typically, these begin with the identification of automatic thoughts—the continuous mental commentary we all experience. Rather than taking these thoughts as accurate reflections of reality, therapy guides you to view them as hypotheses about your circumstances, encouraging you to consider alternative perspectives. This process helps you achieve a more balanced and less distressing view of your troubles.

You may wish to seek clinical therapeutic help with your anger issues. Mindfulness-based therapies may be used that will integrate Buddhist mindfulness meditation practices with traditional cognitive-behavioral methods. Mindfulness works well in anger management. These approaches emphasize the non-judgmental awareness of thoughts and feelings to deal with the root causes of your anger. Examples include:

- **Mindfulness-Based Cognitive Therapy**: Designed to support individuals dealing with frequent episodes of depression and ongoing melancholy. It integrates the fundamentals of cognitive therapy with meditation practices and the development of mindfulness. The goal is to acquaint you with the thought patterns typically linked to mood disorders and assist you in forming a new, more positive relationship with them.
- **Mindfulness-Based Stress Reduction**: Offers in-depth mindfulness training to aid individuals who are struggling with stress, anxiety, depression, and pain. It will employ a mix of mindfulness meditation, bodily awareness, yoga,

and examination of your behavior, thought, emotion, and action patterns.
- **Acceptance and Commitment Therapy**: This form of mindfulness therapy concentrates on maintaining awareness in the present moment and embracing thoughts and feelings without critique. It strives to navigate you through tough emotions, allowing you to invest your energy in recovery rather than fixating on adverse experiences.
- **Dialectical Behavior Therapy**: DBT, a variant of cognitive behavioral therapy (CBT), caters to individuals who experience emotions deeply. It aims to facilitate your understanding and acceptance of challenging emotions, equip you with strategies to control them and support you in implementing positive life changes.

Current studies show these methods can outperform conventional therapy in treating a wide range of issues, such as depression, anxiety, substance misuse, and relationship problems.

MANAGING SADNESS AND DEPRESSION

Sadness is a common emotion sometimes caused by an event or loss. Everyone feels sad sometimes. You may feel sad for different reasons. You may have experienced major life changes or disappointing events. Sadness may cause you to react in different ways. You might cry, listen to sad music, or spend more time alone.

Being sad is a normal reaction in difficult times. But usually, the sadness goes away. When a sad mood lasts for 2 weeks or more and interferes with normal, everyday functioning, you may be depressed.

Symptoms of depression include:

- Feeling sad, empty, or hopeless often or all the time
- Not wanting to do activities that used to be fun
- Weight gain or loss, or changes in appetite
- Trouble falling asleep or staying asleep, or sleeping too much
- Feeling irritable, easily frustrated, or restless
- Lack of energy or feeling tired
- Feeling worthless or overly guilty
- Trouble concentrating, remembering things, or making decisions
- Thinking about suicide or hurting yourself

If you are experiencing several of these symptoms nearly every day for 2 weeks or more, and they interfere with day-to-day activities or cause significant distress, you should talk to your healthcare provider. Things you can do to control and remediate your sadness are:

- **Acknowledge what's happening.** It's OK not to feel OK. If you are feeling sad, know that you are not alone.
- **Take care of yourself.** Eat well, exercise, and rest. Take time for yourself. Acknowledge your successes. You are doing the best you can.
- **Be mindful of how you're feeling.** While doing an activity you enjoy, focus on the here-and-now. Notice how each part of an activity gives you satisfaction, hope, joy, or stress reduction. This can be as simple as staying present while you are making dinner and enjoying each step in that process.

- **Maintain connections with others.** Reach out to people you want to connect with, like your friends, family, neighbors, and co-workers.

If your sadness does not go away, you will want to seek help from a professional. If you think you may be depressed, the first step to seeking treatment is to talk to a healthcare provider. This is especially important if your symptoms are getting worse or affecting your daily activities. Depression is not your fault.

Getting support helps you and your loved ones. Make an appointment with a counselor. If you or someone you know is struggling or in crisis, help is available. Call or text 988 or chat at 988lifeline.org

Individuals with chronic depression often feel detached from their surroundings, leading to a cycle where their actions fail to influence their future behavior positively. A method called Cognitive Behavioral Analysis System of Psychotherapy (CBASP) is uniquely crafted to address this detachment seen in chronic depression. It has been the focus of the most extensive psychotherapy study ever conducted and has proven to be significantly more effective than other treatments for chronic depression.

Early-life maltreatment and trauma can significantly disrupt normal psychological development, leading to early-onset chronic depression. Maltreatment varies widely, encompassing everything from physical abuse to emotional invalidation. This often teaches children from a young age that they cannot depend on others, they must avoid mistakes, or they cannot freely express their thoughts and feelings. These early lessons persist into adulthood, influencing behavior that echoes early childhood experiences. For instance, a child who experienced neglect might grow up to be an adult who avoids relying on others, thereby never experiencing the support of others.

Chronic depression can also emerge in adulthood, triggered by significant life changes like chronic illness, loss, or trauma, leading to prolonged emotional dysregulation. These adults may not have experienced childhood maltreatment but can develop similar unhelpful beliefs, resulting in ongoing feelings of emptiness and depression. Studies have shown that CBASP therapy effectively addresses both early and late-onset chronic depression.

Through CBASP, patients are encouraged to scrutinize the outcomes of their interpersonal actions. By shifting focus from preconceived notions to tangible environmental feedback, individuals start making more accurate predictions about others. This process, known as perceptual reconnection, enhances one's ability to absorb feedback from social interactions, ultimately enriching their relationships. CBASP aims to facilitate more meaningful and rewarding connections through a method called situational analysis.

Situational analysis focuses the patient's attention on the impact of their actions on others and their effects during therapy sessions. By examining challenging social interactions in detail and identifying more constructive responses, individuals learn to align their thoughts and actions with their current environment rather than past traumas. CBASP therapy aims to heal interpersonal trauma by dissecting the patient's past projections and reshaping present relationships for a healthier psychological outlook.

REFERENCES

About Erik Weihenmayer. (n.d.). Erik Weihenmayer. https://erikweihenmayer.com/about-erik/

Aldao, A., Nolen-Hoeksema, S., & Schweizer, S. (2010). Emotion-regulation strategies across psychopathology: A meta-analytic review. *Clinical Psychology Review, 30*(2), 217–237. https://doi.org/10.1016/j.cpr.2009.11.004

Atre, S. et. al. (n.d.). Socialigence. https://www.socialigence.net/blog/social-intelligence-in-research/

Bar-On, R. (2004). The Bar-On emotional quotient inventory (EQ-i): Rationale, description and summary of psychometric properties. In G. Geher (Ed.), *Measuring emotional intelligence: Common ground and controversy* (pp. 115–145). Nova Science Publishers.

Barra, M. (2020, April 26). *9 rare and powerful quotes about the importance of self awareness.* Medium. https://medium.com/skillupped/9-rare-and-powerful-quotes-about-the-importance-of-self-awareness-ebeb1d2ebf

Caruso, D. (n.d.). *David Caruso quotes.* A-Z Quotes. https://www.azquotes.com/quote/579598

Castillo, L. (2023, January 31). *Emotional intelligence statistics [fresh research].* Gitnux. https://blog.gitnux.com/emotional-intelligence-statistics/#:

Celestine, N. (2023). *Abraham Maslow, his theory & contribution to psychology.* PositivePsychology.com. https://positivepsychology.com/abraham-maslow/

Covey, S. (n.d.). *The 7 Habits of Highly Effective People®.* FranklinCovey. https://www.franklincovey.com/the-7-habits/

Disney, W. (2020). *Walt Disney quotes.* BrainyQuote. https://www.brainyquote.com/quotes/walt_disney_163027

Emotional intelligence. (2019, March 23). Emotional intelligence. Wikipedia. https://en.wikipedia.org/wiki/Emotional_intelligence

Emotional intelligence: Why it can matter more than IQ summary. (n.d.). SuperSummary. https://www.supersummary.com/emotional-intelligence-why-it-can-matter-more-than-iq/summary/

Gerald, D. (n.d.). *Drew Gerald quotes.* Goodreads. https://www.goodreads.com/quotes/10014519-look-outside-and-you-will-see-yourself-look-inside-and

Goleman, D. (2023). *4 emotional intelligence skills for trying times.* Korn Ferry. https://www.kornferry.com/insights/briefings-for-the-boardroom/4-emotional-intelligence-skills-for-trying-times/

REFERENCES

Hunt, R. (2011). *Seventy-one percent of employers say they value emotional intelligence over IQ, according to CareerBuilder survey.* (2011, August 18). CareerBuilder Newsroom. https://press.careerbuilder.com/2011-08-18-Seventy-One-Percent-of-Employers-Say-They-Value-Emotional-Intelligence-Over-IQ-According-to-CareerBuilder-Survey

Kihlstrom, J. F., & Cantor, N. (2011). Social intelligence. In R. J. Sternberg & S. B. Kaufman (Eds.), *The Cambridge handbook of intelligence* (pp. 564–581). Cambridge University Press. https://doi.org/10.1017/CBO9780511977244.029

Kim, Alan, "Wilhelm Maximilian Wundt", *The Stanford Encyclopedia of Philosophy* (Winter 2022 Edition), Edward N. Zalta & Uri Nodelman (eds.), URL = <https://plato.stanford.edu/archives/win2022/entries/wilhelm-wundt/>.

Landry, L. (2019, April 3). *Why emotional intelligence is important in leadership.* Harvard Business School Online's Business Insights Blog. https://online.hbs.edu/blog/post/emotional-intelligence-in-leadership

Marenus, M. (2023). *Howard Gardner's theory of multiple intelligences.* Simply Psychology. https://www.simplypsychology.org/multiple-intelligences.html

Payne, W. L. (1985). *A study of emotion: developing emotional intelligence; self- integration; relating to fear, pain and desire* [doctoral dissertation, The Union for Experimenting Colleges and Universities]. ProQuest Dissertations & Theses Global.

Salovey, P., & Mayer, J.D. (1990). Emotional intelligence. *Imagination, Cognition, and Personality, 9*(3), 185–211. https://doi.org/10.2190/

Smith, M., MA. (2023, October 11). *Empathy: how to feel and respond to the emotions of others.* HelpGuide.org. https://www.helpguide.org/articles/relationships-communication/empathy.htm/

The Mayer-Salovey-Caruso emotional intelligence test (MSCEIT). (n.d.). Personality Laboratory at the University of New Hampshire. https://mypages.unh.edu/jdmayer/mayer-salovey-caruso-emotional-intelligence-test-msceit

Tzu, L. (n.d.). *Lao Tzu quotes.* BrainyQuote. https://www.brainyquote.com/quotes/lao_tzu_130742

Valadon, O. (2023, October 18). *What we get wrong about empathic leadership.* Harvard Business Review. https://hbr.org/2023/10/what-we-get-wrong-about-empathic-leadership

Weil, S. (n.d.). *Simone Weil quotes.* Goodreads. https://www.goodreads.com/quotes/522585-attention-is-the-rarest-and-purest-form-of-generosity

Made in the USA
Middletown, DE
23 April 2024